How to Write a Book and Publish in 30 Days
2nd edition

Dr. Jolene Church

ISBN:
ISBN-13: 978-0692139295

HOW TO WRITE A BOOK AND PUBLISH IN 30 DAYS

Printed in North Charleston, SC 29406

USA

Library of Congress Cataloguing- in-Publication Data
Church, Jolene
How to Write a Book and Publish in 30 Days, 2nd ed. by Dr. Jolene Church
ISBN: 978-0692139295

Library of Congress Control Number: 2018912683

Successful Thinking Mindset

DEDICATION

To everyone moved to write. It's time to share your story with the world.

CONTENTS

1. This is perhaps the strangest table of contents that you will ever come across, as it's not technically a table of contents.

2. This is a *non-table* of contents.

3. How to Write a Book and Publish in 30 Days is presented in a day-by-day format.

4. You will read just one chapter each day.

5. Day 1= Chapter 1, Day 2= Chapter 2, etc.

6. This is not a writing mechanics or style manual. Rather, it is a step-by-step process to help you achieve your goal of writing and publishing a book.

7. Throughout the book you will be coached through the process to help you overcome potential pitfalls.

8. The effort that put in is result that you will yield.

9. On Day 30, you should have a published book.

10. What are you waiting for? Let's get started!

ACKNOWLEDGMENTS

There isn't a day that goes by that I do not feel a deep sense of appreciation for my family and friends. It is my love for them that inspires me to new heights and keeps me spreading light.

My kids and grandkids are the joys of my life. They remind me that love is what gives life meaning and purpose.

I thank my mom for being just a super cool mom. Thanks for being a great cheerleader.

I know that my grandmother and grandfather are smiling down from heaven because they know that *I get it.*

To Hawsie and the millionaire lifestyle. I love you.

To Vicki, the core of the creation of this book.

To Claudia, I can't wait to read your first published book!

Finally, I must acknowledge each and every person who has picked up this book and is reading this page. This book was written for you and the inspiration of your unborn dreams and desires served as a catalyst and motivating force for this project. Never ever give up!

INTRODUCTION

After publishing my first book I was inundated with people sharing with me that they "have always had a dream to write a book." The most common statement amongst all of these *would be* authors was "I just don't know where to begin." One of my closest friends was one of these people, so How to Write and Publish a Book in 30 Days was born.

In July 2018, the 1st edition was published, and within just a few weeks, a 2nd edition was needed as the publishing platform that I recommend writers use made some significant changes. Instead of rushing to make changes and re-release, I decided instead to take advantage of this change and learn how to improve my next edition even more. I did this by providing hands on assistance and guidance to prospective authors through their writing process. Those who were up for the 30 day challenge were provided personalized coaching, by me. In addition, word spread fast that I had some "secret sauce" for writing a book and requests for my coaching services poured in. All of a sudden, my book was a bestseller and I was an author incubator. What these experiences did for me was to provide me with additional information to bring you in this new edition because I was able to pinpoint where people get stuck through the process.

Prospective author questions and challenges have helped make this revised edition, more robust, because again and again, common theme problem areas arose with each author. Although no two author's life situations or motivations were the same, the themes that emerged gave me great insight to improve how I guide future writers. I am grateful to all of the authors that I have been blessed to coach and facilitate the incubation of some pretty fabulous projects.

I explained that almost immediately after releasing the 1st edition of this book that the recommended platform changed and therefore, the information provided in the 1st edition was outdated before the ink dried – bummer, but I got over it. I happened to really like the old platform, but I believe that the benefits of using the new platform will really help you in your publishing efforts.

With all this said, let me begin by telling you that just because there was a change in the publishing platform, this does not mean that you cannot still publish for free – because you CAN! What I provide you in this book is the updated step-by-step process using the new platform AND insightful coaching and information so that you can achieve your dream of becoming a published author. Finally, if between this publication and the time you pick up this book, something in the publishing platform changes again, you can always reach out to me through my website at my website www.drjolenechurch.com. I'd not only be happy to assist you in navigating the publishing maze, but I'd also love to hear from you once you complete your project. I LOVE success stories. Also, just because the publishing platform has changed, the HOW TO WRITE A BOOK IN 30 DAYS part has NOT changed. I still provide you with a proven plan to finally get your book completed.

I wish you, patience with the process, grace with yourself, and ultimate success. You've totally got this.

DAY 1

Getting Started

At first, they will ask why you're doing it. Later they'll ask how you did it.

So, you have always wanted to write a book but were never quite sure how to begin, or even what to write about. Let me start by telling you that I get where you are because I've been there too, and I have now helped hundreds of others who have experienced the same thing. The process can seem daunting, but with a bit of guidance on the steps to take, I assure you that it's possible to complete a book in far less time than you would ever imagine.

Let me begin by telling you, this book is not a book on the technical aspects of how to write, but rather how to get started and complete your writing project. Your writing technique and skills, well, that's up to you. All I ask is that you come as you are. If you have a dream, let's make it a reality.

The reason that this book was even created was because my friend, Vicki, and countless others, have expressed to me their desire to write a book. Each of these people shared with me that they "don't know where to begin" or what the publication process entails. For some, they believe self-publishing is expensive, and it can be, but it doesn't have to be. In fact, you can complete your book in little to no money and begin making money in royalties. There are yet others that are *working on* their book (or books), but for whatever reason, they just can't seem to pull everything together to complete the project. There are people out there like Claudia, who have complete, unpublished novels, and pieces of novels, brilliant literary creations, collecting dust. I met Claudia, at the book signing of the 1st edition of this book. At the writing of this 2nd edition, Claudia is up to 13 completed novels and is working on 14! She is currently in the process, of publishing one of her 13 books.

Whichever group you fall into, this book is for you. This is how you take a dream and turn it into reality. This is how you get it done! This is how you get all of your questions answered AND are provided a plan to pull all of the information together, to ensure your success.

Starting with today, Day 1, your journey to become an author has now begun. Just by picking up this book and flipping through the pages, you have taken the first step toward achieving your dream. I'd like you to promise to stick with this program for the next 30 days. No excuses. I don't even want to hear, "Okay, my Day 1 will be tomorrow, or Monday." Today is the first day of your becoming a published author in 30 days. It is my job to guide you through the process in an easy foolproof process. All I need from you is for you to give yourself 30 days to prove to yourself that you *can* accomplish this goal. I also ask that you give yourself grace if you slip. Simply dust yourself off and get back to it.

Let me forewarn you that you WILL have setbacks. Life will happen. You may experience fear and doubt, questioning whether you should even be attempting this feat, but I assure you, this is totally achievable and you CAN do this! Fear, doubt or other's defeating comments can be take the wind out of your sails if you allow it. You are worthy of accomplishing your dream and you have a solid, proven plan to make it happen in your toolkit.

A total bonus is that I am bringing you this instructional book, not only from the perspective that I too had the same dream as you, to write a book, but I am also bringing this to you as a success coach. Why a *'How To'* by a success coach? Perhaps I'm a wee bit biased, but I can't think of a better pairing!

If you think about it, it makes great sense. I have successfully coached hundreds of clients over the years to help them shift their lives into the direction they desire. I have also coached people just like you, people with a dream to write a book. Who better to help motivate you and encourage you along the way than a success coach? Let's face it, life gets in the way, but all too often we get in our own way. Specifically, our thinking gets in our way. We overthink from an overly critical perspective, not realizing that the only thing that holds us back is our mindset.

Over the past several years, I have become what is known as an author incubator, helping people, just like you, take those ideas that are on fire in their soul, become their own literary masterpiece. There are so many possible interruptions that could thwart your ability to write your book, and the greatest barrier is often inside your head. I help you to incubate and birth those ideas, smashing down barriers and reaching the successful outcome that you desire.

In my book, *Thinking 101: Fundamentals of a Successful Mindset*, I explain how barriers develop within our thinking inhibit our success. We continually impose new barriers on ourselves without even realizing what we are doing. Writing the book that you have always wanted to write, especially whipping it out in 30 days, will require that any barriers that pop up along the way be crushed. For this reason, this book is designed to help coach you to desired results.

Again, challenges will arise and new mountains will instantly emerge throughout the process, impeding your ability to move forward. I am here to tell you, there is no mountain that cannot be scaled or winnowed down to a molehill. It is your determination and willingness to persevere and your dedication to what you desire that will lead you to the victory you seek.

Maybe you have an epic story in your mind and you just need to figure out how to get it out of your head, onto paper, and into the hands of others. Maybe you are like Donna who has a story that needs to be heard. Maybe you are like Jeff who has immense industry knowledge and wants to share that knowledge to help others.

Whatever your quandary over the process or where to begin, you are on the right track by searching out *how to* answers and then immediately applying that knowledge. Just simply knowing how is not enough. If it were simply Googling *how to* you would have no excuse to not have written your book. The key to writing is that you need to get writing.

It's far too easy to simply not start, because you have no clue how to even begin, but as I will show you, it's not so bad. It is my intention to help you push past the starting line, guiding you straight to the finish to the dream that you have long visualized.

I will also help you stay off of the rabbit trails, which are actually manifested actions of procrastination based from fear. I've got your back on this. I will help you stay on the straight and narrow, sharing my insight, my own challenges that I have faced, as well as the challenges that I have witnessed in the authors that I have coached.

What you will gain over the next 30 days is far more than a completed book. I'm excited to be a part of your writing process and your results. You can definitely expect greater confidence and a sense of empowerment. A big part of tapping into your confidence and empowerment will be found in your dedication and perseverance. You can also expect to gain an understanding that you can do anything by believing, gaining knowledge, learning from disappointment, and pushing forward no matter what.

Remember, *if you fail to learn, you learn to fail.* Your willingness to be honest with yourself when you are trying to make excuses and learn from the days that you struggle to string three words together, let alone the days you fail to hit word count will make all the difference in your outcome. Self-defeating thoughts become rooted into how you feel about the process and your actions will align with how you feel. To illustrate this, imagine that you have to clean a garage, packed with junk and you dread doing it. Will you procrastinate? Put it off? It's highly likely you won't go bounding out to the garage full of energy with an excited, "Let's do this!" No, instead you would probably mope out into the garage with a thought, "Ugh! I don't want to do this!"

There will be some really tough days. You will be tired. You won't want to write. You will question what you are doing. This is normal. My advise is to keep moving forward despite these thoughts and the associated feelings. You get to create new thoughts and new feelings.

You will gain the information that you are unclear on and obtain the inspiration that you need to help guide you toward achieving your goal of writing and publishing your very own book. Yes, you can be an author, and if you follow this 30-day program, you will be a published author in just one month.

I realize that you probably have many questions and that you would like to fast forward to the answers. Again, I've been just where you are. I was in search of answers. How much does it cost to get published? Do I need to have an agent or go through a publishing house? How do I go about editing, creating a cover, or formatting the book? I assure you that I will answer these questions and put your mind at ease.

If you are worried about costs to publish, I'm here to tell you it isn't going to cost thousands or even hundreds of dollars. Publishing can cost next to nothing, and I'm going to guide you through the entire process. Don't think that money is a barrier. It's not. You are the only barrier that you need to deal with. Once you get past any non-productive thoughts, you are golden.

Promise me this, that you will not entertain thoughts that don't serve you. If they don't feel good about the thoughts you are having, let's chuck 'em! If you do this, I can promise you that you will have a much more enjoyable experience, because you will only hold on to thoughts that help you move forward – and that feels so good. It's those good feelings that are going to motivate you and keep you going, because your thoughts contribute to your feelings, and your feelings contribute to your actions and then your results.

Don't let what you don't know make you think that you can't.

Other than unknowns about the process, a very common hang-up for many potential authors is self-doubt. Doubt cripples our productive thinking, and it will paralyze the manifestation of your book-writing dream. Another hang-up is thinking that you aren't good enough, or that all literary art must meet some rigorous criteria. To that I proclaim, "HOGWASH"! And to the pompous, arrogant, literary *know-it-alls*, shame on you for censoring dream manifestation and imagination. Future authors, you *are* good enough. Let's take a moment to let this sink in because it's extremely important.

You are the only you. The story that you have is *your* story. It doesn't matter what it is, it's your unique creation. You are an awesome creation and from creation, let creation happen. You have this burning desire in you. It's your flame; let your flame glow brightly!

It may be true that not every literary work will become a best-seller or classic work, but it is *your* work, *your* dream, and nobody can take that away from you. There will likely be haters and harsh critics. Don't pay them any regard or let that keep you from moving forward. Hold on to the glory that you can and will achieve your goal. Don't allow that flame inside of you to be extinguished.

It's a rush when you see your book in print. I want you to achieve that. I want you to feel that rush. It is a feeling that never gets old as an author. With each new book, I feel the same amazing feeling as I hold the first printed version. I want you to experience that pride that arises when you see your name on the cover of your book. I want you to feel the joy of signing a copy of your book for someone. As I lead you through this journey, I will train you to identify when limiting thoughts pop up and how to stop them in their tracks and crush them.

I think this is a good point for you to stop right here. I'd like you to think about what it will feel like to hold your printed book. Seriously, stop what you are doing and think about your printed book. I want you to envision it. Think of yourself holding your book and flipping to the first page where you see your name as the author. Turn the pages in your mind. Look at the copyright page, the dedication, and the first chapter. Let that soak in. Close your eyes for a moment and imagine yourself flipping through the pages.

Now, what does your cover look like? Is there a picture? Is it simply the title on a solid color background? Where is your name printed? At the top or bottom of the cover? How thick is your book? How many pages do you see your book being?

Now imagine receiving a box in the mail filled with several dozen copies of your book. Imagine cutting open the package and as you open up the box to reveal the contents. Imagine the feeling when you see the cover of your book. Do you have a smile on your face? Is there someone you want to show first? Or give a copy to first? Hold in your mind the image of you showing off your book to the person from your vision. Focus on the smile on your face and the joyous feeling.

Now that you have created the experience, it is so. There is a gap between where you are right now, thinking about writing a book and the experience that you just felt and saw in your mind. This book is how you build a bridge to get over the gap as it provides you with the steps needed to get you to your destination, living what you just felt as you imagined your experience.

For me, writing and publishing my books have provided such fulfilling and rewarding experiences as I have turned a dream into reality. I vividly remember dreaming up the concept of my first book and rushing home to share my idea with my daughters. My excitement was contagious and as I shared ideas, they added to my ideas of what I might include in my book. I remember holding the first copy of my very first book. I felt so excited, I thought I was going to burst. I couldn't wait for my daughter to get home so that I could show her.

It's not all about the rush though. Yes, it's exciting, dopamine is a great feel-good hormone, but there is something so much more that I can't wait for you to experience for yourself. Through my writing, I have been able to share ideas and add to others' new ideas, dreams, and thinking processes. This is exciting for me as it is my mission to inspire others, especially inspiring people to dream. That being said, I would like to address your motives and what's driving you so that we can establish a foundation and help you create a successful outcome.

The Driving Force

Let me start by asking you the question, why do you want to write? Would you like to leave a legacy for your children? Do you aspire to be the next J.K. Rowling? Do you simply love sharing stories or teaching? Understanding your motivation is an important part of this process. Being able to dig deep and be reflective and honest as to why you want to write is necessary, as that motivation is what will help you persevere to the finish line.

Not only do I write and publish my own books, but I am also a ghost writer. Helping someone develop and articulate their story is always exciting, but again, it's the coach in me that thrives on this. I dive into the motivation of these storytellers and help them maintain a source of fire and passion to get their stories on paper.

When I am conducting life coaching or executive coaching sessions, I use reflective exercises with my clients to help them "get real" with themselves. I go into great detail on this "getting real" process in my book, *Allowing Inspired Transformation: 6 Steps to Define Your Purpose for an Epic Effect*. Being completely honest with yourself is essential for you to overcome any challenges. For example, if you were to say, "I want to write a book so that I can become a millionaire" my question for you would be why? What does that mean to you? What would being a millionaire do for you? Does it mean financial freedom? If so, now we are on to something as we are truly driving into your core and what is most important to you. When we work from our core, work doesn't feel like work and we will push hard.

Critics might say that your chances of becoming the next big author are slim to none, but this doesn't matter. When it comes to your dreams and desires, what someone else believes is *their* belief. It doesn't need to be yours. The fact that you are trying to be honest with your motivation is the most important thing. Your motivation is a driving force that we can use to your advantage. Your motivation will also be your armor against derailment.

Let's go back to the example of being a millionaire author for a moment. From a psychological perspective, we could scrutinize your motivation to death, or we identify potential landmines that we can navigate around. If money or fame is the driving force is the driving force, might pursuit of money over passion get in the way of your story? It certainly could, and this would be a potential landmine for you, but it's also going to drive you to keep going. You desire to be rich and there is nothing wrong with that. You must understand, however, that writing is not like the movie *Field of Dreams*. Just because you write the story doesn't mean the readers will come. Let this sink in, because I'm certain there is much more to your desire to write a book, than pursuing money—I guarantee it!

I'm not saying that money as a motivator is bad at all. I would never discourage anyone from seeking wealth, financial freedom, and abundance. Look at how many people choose careers based on potential earnings. However, becoming a best-selling author is a bit different than choosing a career that has an established market rate.

If you know that you have a book idea that will be a hit and you want to sell a lot of books, I recommend that you get all the feedback and editing that you can get, be ready to roll up your sleeves and come up with a dynamic marketing strategy, not only for your book, but for you as well.

It certainly won't be easy, but is it possible? Absolutely! Anything is possible. There are some great stories of people who have guerilla-marketed their books to success, but these really are the exception, not the rule. Knowing this, you can overcome a landmine in thinking that you will automatically have fans just because you wrote a book with a catchy title. Of course, you may think that your catchy title or compelling cover will *surely grab the attention of readers*, but that may not be so. So why even try? Because you want to and you can!

You must believe in your work and that your story is the story of all stories. From self-help to historical or science-fiction, your passion for your topic or story is what will keep you going and give your book depth. Your passion for what you believe will drive you and will help you articulate how your work stands out from the rest. Just walk through any book store or library and you can't help but be humbled. It's not cocky that you need to be, it's in touch with your core, your motivations because this will make all the difference in the world in how you shine. I don't want to discourage you in any way, instead I'd like you to dig into the meaning of what's motivating you—hint: it's really not just the money.

Motivation is an amazing force. The reasons why we do things and the drive behind our desires is fascinating. Although this is a book on How to Write A Book, the concept of motivation is important to understand at the onset of your writing endeavor. If you don't understand why you want what you want, it will be too easy to make up excuses why you can't.

Let's pull back the curtain from the fame and fortune thing. You see, for some reading this book, fame and fortune didn't even come to mind as motivation. Yet for others, this is a primary motivator. What is important to understand is that we all have a natural desire to succeed and thrive. This drive goes deeper than our caveman ancestors' drive to survive, but it is very much related. It is in the composition of our cells to thrive. Motivation is in your cells and your inner being is striving to succeed. It needs to be born. Creation cannot be stopped.

Success means something different to everyone. For some it means money. For others, it means happiness, security, personal fulfillment. For artists, and of course writers are artists, success is typically realized when they can share their expression and others can participate in it. A musician is a great example of this. A pianist may play and experience pleasure and fulfillment through the expression of a song in solitude, but if another person listens and comments on the beauty of the performance, the artist feels a sense of completeness in the artistic expression because of the affirmation of what the artist finds fulfilling. If a musician becomes famous doing what her or she loves, yes it may be cool and a bonus, but the real drive and motivation is the music. Writing is that. It is an instrument of expression appreciated in varying degrees by others or not at all. But it's the act of expressing that is key. The fulfillment from expression of one's authentic self is a divine reward and is what this life is all about.

We were born to thrive; it is a natural. Motivation, whatever is driving you to thrive and achieve, must be embraced. An example I gave earlier as a reason someone might want to write a book is to leave a legacy for their children. They want to leave something that their loves ones will be proud to share with other family members for generations to come. "Your great-grandfather wrote this book." There is pride in the thought of having a bigger purpose and contribution from life layered in this reason. It feels good to think that your family and future generations might share your story and are proud of you. Understanding this, every time you come up with an excuse as to why you are not writing or following the next step in the 30-day program, think of what motivated you in the first place. What is your success factor? What is that motivation? Or maybe there is a person that inspires you to fulfill this desire.

Now for a shocker and something that you would have likely never guessed! I am not simply telling you how to write a book in 30 days, I actually did this with the first edition of this book. Yes, the book you are reading right now was written in 30 days. The same tips, principles, and exercises that will guide you through the process were used to write this book.

Enough dilly-dallying. Let's get on with this writing thing already!

Day 1 Exercise

Day 1 begins with a *pre-writing exercise*, even though it's really not "pre" anything. For this exercise and others throughout the 30 days, you will need a notepad (I may refer to this as your writing journal) and a pen. This book is set up with an exercise every day for 30 days that will contribute to a final product. Please don't try to skip steps or do multiple-day exercises in one day. It's important to do one exercise every day.

The pre-writing exercise is something that you are going to come back to throughout the process and in some cases expand upon, so it is crucial that you put your best effort forward. The more you put into this, the better the outcome. Disregard the distractions of your mind as you begin wondering whether you are doing it right or not. That's just your ego getting in your way.

Your ego is the only thing standing between you and your dream. Think about it. Anytime you desired something strongly and had to have it now or had to have more, what was that? It was a little thought in your head saying, "I want this now," or "I wanted *this* much, but now that I have that, I want even more." That is your ego, never satisfied.

You will never be good enough to your ego. If your ego decides to tell you how great you are and superior you are to others, then watch out for the ensuing trap! It is your ego's job to mess with your successful thinking. Do not let your ego get in your way.

I had you visualize your book and the feeling that you would have holding your book for a reason. That excitement is your defense against ego. You see, joy is rooted in love. When you are operating in a feeling and place of love, judgement and arrogance cannot take hold and trap you. You are a writer. Protect your creativity from self-doubt and judgement. Focus on your joy. Keep your joy fresh in your mind every single day when you start your writing exercise for the next 30 days. It will only take a few minutes. Slow down, visualize, and feel the joy.

Are you ready? If you answered yes, let's get started on your first task. Open your notebook to the first page and write the following questions/statements and answer them as thoroughly as you can. Spend some time on this. This is the building block for Day 2. Let's begin. When you are done with this, you can come back to it and add to it, but DO NOT move on to Day 2 until tomorrow. Deal? Alright.

Answer the following questions:

1. Month/Day/Year?

2. Book Title? (Don't worry if you don't have a clue. Come up with a working title that pops into your head).

3. My book is about… (Whether fiction or non-fiction, write a brief description about your book that would entice someone to want to read it. Again, don't get hung up on perfection, just tell yourself, on paper, about your book).

4. My motivation for writing this book is…. (Don't shortchange

yourself here, tell your story. Why do you want to write a book and why *this* book?).

5. Who would be interested in this book and why? (Explain a bit about your audience. I can't tell you how important this is, so really ask yourself why someone would want to read your book).

6. The cover of my book will have…. (What's it going to look like on the front? On the back? Will your photo be on the back with your bio? Or will you have excerpts from the book? Visualize it. Describe your dream book design).

7. My book will be dedicated to…. (Who would you like to dedicate your book to and why?).

Get Ready

For your *Day 2 Exercise* you will need 3 x 5 index cards, a marker, and a pen or pencil.

DAY 2

Either you run the day, or the day runs you. – Jim Rohn

Welcome to Day 2! Can you believe that you are now a full day into your 30-day program? Well, believe it, you are on your way to becoming a published author. Yes, just 29 days left, and you will have accomplished your dream. We will begin Day 2 with a review of your Day 1 exercise, beginning with Question #3.

My book is about… What to write about can often be a stumbling block. Congratulations on articulating your topic and some details about your book. If for some reason you didn't provide much of a detailed answer for Question #3 yesterday, please take a moment before reading on to elaborate your answer, providing yourself with as much information as possible. You can even write the answer as if you are being interviewed by a talk show host. Make the host excited about your book.

Selecting your topic and genre is somewhat influenced by what you hope to accomplish by writing. Is it just to tell a great story? To help others? Or to entertain? We first need to look at the big picture and what your vision is for your writing so that we can hone in on your topic. Let me add that you may already know exactly what you want to write on, but understanding why is an important step to getting you to your goal—becoming a published author.

Why do you want to write a book? Think about this question. Is it just a goal on your bucket list? What makes it so important? Really put some thought into this.

If it is simply a desire, what is so appealing about it? Do you believe that you will feel like you accomplished something? Think about that *something*, what is it? Do you feel that there is something in you that must be shared? Do you believe that by writing a book that you will feel that you have fulfilled some destiny or greater purpose?

For me, I always wanted to write a book. I couldn't really pinpoint why; it was just a strong desire. I would think 'what would I write about if I were to write a book?' I'd think, 'I could write a novel or share knowledge on something that I know something about, but what did I know that would be of value to someone else?' I'd ask myself 'I'm a mother of four; what do I really know?'

I easily could have written a book on my life experiences, on parenthood, or on the quest for a topic to write a book. There was no limit to potential topics. I just knew that I had to write. I didn't know about what, but I knew that I was missing part of the equation and that was why. What was it that was compelling me to write? It was when I connected my purpose that the topics came flooding to me, and the stories connected.

My purpose is to inspire, passion, confidence and authenticity. Can you see why I'm writing this book? Can you see how once I connected to my purpose, what to write on became clear?

Being honest with why you want to write in the first place is a crucial initial step. Your topic must be near and dear to you. Don't be critical of any book idea that you have. My suggestion is to make a list! Every time you have a book idea or a topic or story that you want to make sure you include, jot it down in your writing journal. I like to record these ideas as memos using the voice recorder on my phone. This is especially helpful when I'm commuting. I may not be able to write while I'm driving, but I can record thoughts as they come so that I don't lose them. The most important point is, get the idea out of your head and recorded somewhere, whether by voice or pen.

Once you have the heart of your book in mind, you are ready to begin.

The Writing Process Begins:
Index Card Exercise

What are the main points that you shared about your book? Take out your index cards and for each point that you shared, write the point in pen or pencil, not the marker; the marker will be used in another step.

This book is about how to write a book in 30 days. What are my main points? The cards that I used for the development of this book are illustrated in Figure 1.

Figure 1- *Index Cards*

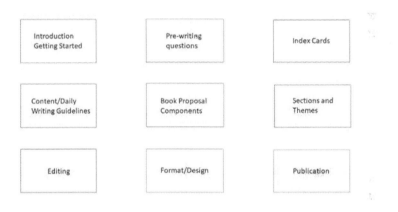

Your index cards will become pieces of your book so start with main topics, points, plots, or themes. In my example, I have broken down some of the elements that I will be covering in this book. Create as many cards as you need to have a separate thought on each card.

For one client that I provided ghost-writing services, I had him write a card for each short story that he wanted to include. The index card only contained a few notes about each story so that it would jog his memory. For example, for a romance novel, you might want to tell a back story of your main character that impacted their ability to give in to love. On an index card you might write something like,

"Heartbroken Jane from Jack's betrayal." On another card you might have, "When she least expected, Mark appeared." And on yet another, "The mountain getaway." Each card will help you to build your story, expand upon your writing, and will help you arrange your book.

Today your focus is on index cards. Create as many cards as you can. Write a point, a concept, a story, a character, or a concept on each card. Strive for no less than 30-40 cards. When you have completed creating your cards, lay them out on a table or on the floor where they won't be disrupted. Stand back and look at your creation.

How do you feel? Overwhelmed? More confused? Are you thinking, "How the heck is this going to turn into a book in 29 more days"?

Reflect back to the reason why you want to write a book. Think about this. How will you feel when you accomplish what you want? Reimagine your vision of your completed book. The mail comes, you cut open the box, and there it is. Search for the joy. Tap into that feeling. Imagine yourself showing someone your book, seeing your book in a bookstore or online, or signing a copy for a dear friend. How does that feel? Pretty darned good, right? Alright, now you are in the right frame of mind for the final task for today.

Look at your index cards and group subjects or items that make sense to be together with similar cards. Perhaps you decide to group your characters together or components of each topic together. Remember, there is no right or wrong. Your goal is to arrange your cards into 10 groups. Put the main topic or point on the top of each grouping stack.

If you are writing fiction and chose to group characters together, have your main character on top, with other characters in declining order of significance to the story. Again, there is no right or wrong way to do this, it is just important that you find some sort of method to group your cards.

Once you have all of your cards arranged into 10 groups you are done for the day. If you later realize that you forgot to include something, you can simply create additional cards and make sure that you also categorize these for use tomorrow.

Lay out your stacks of cards and have good look at your top index card for each stack. Tomorrow we will begin where we left off. You should be proud of your accomplishment, you have nearly completed the outline for your book.

DAY 3

Keep your face always toward the sunshine – and shadows will fall behind you. –
Walt Whitman

Your Day 2 exercise was to construct bits and pieces of your book so that we can put together an outline. Today we are going to make some sense out of what you compiled. Yesterday you made index cards for various topics, stories, or characters. Today you are going to think about your book, using the index cards that you created, with some structure. After that, we are going to expand on the structure and framework to help you visualize flow and content. But first let's do a check in.

Where Are You?

Where are you in the process right now? Even more confused than when you first picked up the book? After all, you have stacks of cards that seem to make no sense, and I left you hanging saying that you nearly completed the outline for your book! Don't worry, let's make sure that we have you mentally prepared for your next big accomplishment – a content embellished outline.

Where are you in your thinking? This is Day 3. I need you to understand that this process is going to rapidly unfold, and you will quickly realize that what you thought was daunting and scary is really not so. In just a few weeks, you are going to be so freaking excited as you near completion of your book. 'Scariness' is just in our thinking, not in reality. Scary is your mind making up stories of what hasn't happened. On a positive note, if your mind is so great at coming up with creating stories, you are well on your way to success as creating a story is exactly what you need to get done! Let's put that mind to better use with something productive.

Look at your current circumstance. You bought this book, you read Day 1 and said, "Why not?" You bought the book and are still here with me because something inside you said, "This is what I want, the author says that she will help me succeed, why not?"

I concur! Why not? If others have done it, why not you?

Your current circumstance is, you are in Day 3. DAY 3 as an author! How cool is that?! Think about it. 'I'm an author!' Does it feel real? Do you believe it? If not, let's re-phrase into something that you can accept and that you will believe. How about, "I'm working on a 30-day writing program to become a published author. I'm putting in the work to write a book."

Unfortunately, self-critical thinking has a tendency to sneak in as you make such powerful statements and then all of a sudden, "What makes you think you can do that?" Or "I really doubt that anyone can truly finish a book in 30 days."

These may be the thoughts that creep in to your head, but you get to decide that you are not accepting those thoughts. Instead, you are going to find a thought that feels real to you, something that you can accept and believe. Let's assume that you are good with, "I'm working on a 30-day writing program to become a published author." How does this statement make you feel? This is an important question because what you think about your circumstance and how you feel about that thought is what will drive your success.

How does it feel to know that you are in a 30-day program and at the end you will be a published author? Pretty flipping good, right? If you don't feel excitement in your gut, keep thinking about that, visualizing showing off your book. Keep visualizing until your feeling changes to excitement. If you feel fear, just remember, anxiety and excitement are both the same energy, shift that anxiety to excitement through a re-focus to your joyful vision.

Writing this book is in your control. Don't fear yourself. Don't fear your success. This is an easy win! Seize it. Now let's get writing!

Organizing Your Thoughts

The purpose of the index cards are to think through what you want in your book. For example, I want a chapter that tells a certain story, and another that tells another story. Finally, I want to have these two stories have a nexus in another chapter when a certain event happens. Or maybe the nexus is when two character's stories cross. By knowing what elements that you want in your book, you can develop a rough outline.

Your stacks of card groups from yesterday may or may not be in groups that could be considered chapters. If you made cards for characters and have a group of all characters, you will need find a place for each of these people. If, on the other hand, you created cards with topics (similar to the example of the cards I illustrated for this book) then your task will be to determine the best order.

Your index cards are chapter content in a very rudimentary form. You will have a main index card for each chapter. Take out your marker and number each top card in chapter order. Beginning with one for Chapter 1 through ten, designate the order of your main cards by marking the chapter number on the main card. For ease of your first book, I suggest that you follow my ten-chapter formula. After numbering the main cards, arrange the cards in order by chapter number. You will have a main card for each chapter designated with the chapter number and you will have associated cards for each chapter. I like to number the support cards in pencil just in case I want to use those points in another chapter instead of where I originally thought.

Each of your outlined thoughts have support behind them. If you put each thought on an index card, you will have plenty of supporting thoughts to pull from as you write. Not only are these talking points within your chapter, but in many cases these will be the subtopics of each section.

The beauty of putting your thoughts on index cards is that you can visualize your book chapters and rearrange them easily. You can assemble your book in front of you on the table, your desk, or even kitchen counter. It's exciting to see how just a bullet point topic on each card instantly transforms into a book that you can visualize. When you have 10 index cards arranged in front of you, with chapter numbers assigned, there is something gratifying, tangible, and exciting about this book-writing-thing actually becoming a reality. By tomorrow you are really going to be feeling it!

Your assignment today is to look over the cards that you developed. Do you need to add main topic cards? Once you have 10 main topics (your chapters), it's time to develop as many coordinating or supporting thoughts and ideas as you can. You may have a pretty good start on this from yesterday. Today, we need to put this in some sort of order.

After you have arranged the main topic cards in front of you with supporting cards to each chapter topic underneath, it's time to expand your thinking. Look at each card. What point do you want to cover or story do you want to tell? Write it on the back of the card. You may end up with one or several examples listed. Make sure to write as much detail as you can fit. Full sentences are best as they will jog your memory later when you go back to look at the card.

It really doesn't matter whether you are writing non-fiction or fiction, the process is the same. In fact, when I was ghost-writing a fictional project, I found this process really fun as I was able to probe the author for important points and storylines that he did not want to forget to include under each specific topic or chapter. This really helped develop a rich storyline. In non-fiction, it helps keep you focused, on task, keeps things organized, and helps you link concepts from one chapter to the next together.

Take your time adding additional cards as needed, rearranging your 10 main cards, and jotting down notes to correspond to each point that you list on each card. At the end of this exercise you will have created a fully annotated outline of your book! Enjoy this part—this is going to help you organize your thoughts and boost your confidence. You have already begun the writing process – no need for butterflies.

Get Ready

Have your computer, pen and paper, or whatever you will be using to write your book handy tomorrow!

"The starting point of all achievement is desire." – Napoleon Hill

DAY 4

"If you are not willing to risk the usual, you will have to settle for the ordinary."

Over the last three days you have taken a desire and have begun to transform it into reality. You pondered what you could possibly write on and then expanded that to an annotated outline, which is your chapter structure and then some. Now it's time to expand on what you have as we begin a deeper conversation around your cards. But first, let's take a moment to check in. First, I need you to do the following:

Lay out your stacks of cards. Ask yourself as yourself if the chapter order that you assigned still seems like it makes the most sense. Remember, each top card is the main point or story of each chapter, and you should have 10 chapters. Underneath each top card you will have all of the additional cards that you developed yesterday.

The first thing that I would like to say is, BRAVO! You really should be very proud that you are at the mid-point of the first week aimed toward accomplishing your dream. Think back to before you started and all the questions that you had. Even though it may not be evident to you right at this moment how you will accomplish this task in just 26 days, the fact is that you just completed a major part of your book. Many people who set out to write a book and fail have skipped this crucial step. And you accomplished it within your first three days! Pat yourself on the back—you deserve it.

I know you are anxious to get started, but I want to make sure that you are focused. Remember that little thing I told you that was so important on Day 1? What? You forgot already? Why are you doing this? Why do you want to write this book? As you stare at your stacks of index cards, your chapters, think about why this book is so important? Now realize you have all of the chapters of your book sitting right in front of you! It's a pretty darned good feeling. Hold on to that feeling and let's get started.

Take a look at your top card. This should be the main point, theme, or story of the chapter. Write at top of each top card a title for the chapter. You may change it later, but let's give each chapter a *working title*. You working title is going to help keep you on point and it will also help you identify if any of your support cards in the stack would be better suited in another stack. Rearrange the cards in the stacks if need be and then we can begin.

Are you happy with your stacks? Do you believe that you have all of the points and supporting thoughts listed on your cards? If not, take the time you need to complete this task. The next step will help you to refine what you have even more. What you will need is your computer, if that is how you will be writing your book, or your notebook. Whatever you are going to be using to write your book, get it out now and let's get to work. You have two tasks; here they are.

#1- Sell Your Book

Open a new Word document or turn to a fresh page in your writing journal. I'd like you to write in a paragraph or two about your book as if you are doing a radio interview. Pretend the interviewer welcomes you to the show and says,

"Welcome to the show. Can you tell the audience about your book? What is it that they will find especially interesting about your book? How does it differ from other books on the same topic or in the same genre?"

Your job here is to sell your book. Give it your best sales pitch as if you were just given five minutes with a celebrity host to tell them how great your book is. You may also want to include why you felt compelled to write the book. Develop your imaginary sales pitch, as you explain whatever is unique about your book and write the sales pitch down. This only needs to be a paragraph or two.

#2- Continue the Conversation

You developed an annotated outline of all of your chapters by writing down information on your index cards and grouping them. Now it is time to expand on that conversation and get writing.

Let's get started with Chapter 1. Open another Word document or a new sheet of paper in the handy typewriter. Begin by writing or typing Chapter 1, followed by your working title. Lay out your Chapter 1 index cards so that you can see all of the points and other information that you wrote out. How do you want to begin? What story, character, or point do you want to introduce first?

Your goal is to write a minimum of 1500 words today. If you are unfamiliar with Microsoft Word, the word count is at the bottom left corner of the screen or you can go to the Review tab and select Word Count from the top ribbon.

The information that you put on each card should be used to elaborate and create content. Imagine yourself explaining why you wrote that point down on the card, if you think about your writing as having a conversation and explaining yourself, it is much easier to get started. Begin writing.

Don't worry about your spelling errors or grammar. Focus on the topic or story information from your Chapter 1 index cards. Don't worry about including information for each of your Chapter 1 card notes. Rome wasn't built in one day and neither is your chapter -it's built in two.

See you on Day 5!

Fulfillment of your dreams is now.

DAY 5

To succeed in life, you need two things: ignorance and confidence. — Mark Twain

Many of us have seen movies where a writer is posed in front of a typewriter, sequestered away from the distractions of life in a quaint little writer's retreat on a mountain top or in a remote beachfront cottage. A cup of coffee or tea sits beside the typewriter and the budding author stares at the blank page. Finally, mustering up enough courage, the writer begins, "Chapter 1," and then a pause.

Let me just say, it helps to get away from distractions, but don't think that you need to go on hiatus from society to write a book. You will know what feels right for you, such as if you need a quiet space or a space with white noise. Believe me, even if there are no distractions, there will come a point over the next few weeks that you distract yourself.

Daily Check In

Your daily check-in is the perfect time for you to journal your responses. Benefits of journaling are: greater clarity and insight gained through reflection and off-loading of any limited thoughts. In addition, when you look back through your journal after you complete this project, you will be able to assess any areas where you struggled or excelled as a part of your overall continual improvement and ongoing learning.

How do you believe you did on Day 4? How did it feel to finally get writing as you used your cards to begin the process? How did it feel to take the ideas that you jotted down, connecting them to your writing? Did you struggle with what to write, or did it flow? How many words did you write? Did you experience *the pause*? For some *the pause* typically comes right after they type "Chapter 1" and for others, it occurs after the first line or first few paragraphs.

I like to tell new authors not to worry about how amazing the first line or first paragraph is. Some people get so hung up on having a riveting opening that they get stuck. Just beginning is the hardest part. Don't let anything stop you from your progress, such as self-doubt or perfectionism. You can go back and change things. **Just write**. It gets easier, and after habitually sitting down and writing every day for an hour (or longer) at a time for a few weeks, it is going to come easier for you. It begins to be something that you look forward to and that you want to dedicate more and more time to. Just know that things that feel difficult in the beginning get easier with practice.

The daily habit that you are building will pay off. Imagine if you were trying to lose weight or get fit. Daily habits, small things that you commit to doing every day, are what will enable you to succeed. This writing process is a daily habit that supports your goal of completing your book.

Again, your success is dependent on your ability to commit to your daily writing habit so that you don't allow yourself to be a perfectionist in your punctuation or grammar as you begin to write. Wondering if you should or should not be using a comma or the proper tense of a verb can derail you. This can be addressed later – and like I tell my husband, that's what editors are for. The key is to get the thoughts from head to paper without distracting, limiting, or judging thoughts derailing you from this task. Just "Get 'er done"!

Keep in mind that some of your chapters will be easier than others. As you get writing, some of your chapters will be longer or shorter than others. What's important is that you think through the basics of what you want to include in your chapter and simply get it out of your head.

On Day 4, you began writing content, at least 1,500 words of content. Your goal is for each chapter to be somewhere between 3,000 and 6,000 words. It's perfectly fine if your chapters are larger, but for a 30-day book project, a 30,000 to 60,000-word book, once formatted, will translate somewhere in the range of 90-180 pages. Pretty impressive for a first book! So relax. Once you get the feel of what 1,500 words feels like, the pressure of writing each day will dissipate.

A major benefit of using the index card system for developing your chapters is that you can keep your cards on you at all times. Each chapter is an index card, so you can carry your entire book in your back pocket, purse, or briefcase! Wrap a rubber band around them or use a large clip and you are good to go! Talk about convenient, especially when you have that *ah-ha* moment when standing in line at the grocery store or while waiting to pick up your kids from school. You can just whip out your "book", aka index cards, and jot down your ideas. In your next writing session, as you lay out your cards, you have additional information already noted on a card tied to a particular chapter.

As you can imagine, a small, pocket-size notebook could work well also, though I'd encourage you to keep as many of your ideas on the index cards because you won't have to gather together several sources to begin writing. Keep it simple and organized. What's important is clearing excuses that could pose barriers to your writing each day. If you can't begin because you forgot your notebook at work or in the car, BOOM, an excuse for delay is born. That is why for this book, I suggest that you use your index cards as a convenient tool to take advantage of each time your mind releases new ideas and keep them with you at all times. Ideas are likely to come while doing the most random activities and you will be ready to capture them.

Another word of advice for using your index cards—don't overthink it! Don't overthink or question yourself if you are doing it correctly. You are simply capturing thoughts that will easily get lost if you don't stop and write them down. Overthinking is a killer of productivity. The important thing is to start by documenting anytime a thought comes. I can't tell you how many times that I have had a thought for a book, blog, or podcast and told myself that I would **definitely remember** the idea and then I got busy and I struggled to recall the exact original idea. Documenting the flow of the ideas when you are in the flow is crucial. Don't wait because you risk losing it.

Back to yesterday's writing. It is very easy, when first beginning to write, to burden yourself with structure and rules. This isn't a time for perfection or beauty. This is a time for you to think about what you want to say. Again, overthinking will cause procrastination—let's crush it immediately. We want to make every moment productive.

Day 5 is an exciting time. You are at a minimum 1,500 words toward the completion of a book. When you strive to write no less than 1,500 words in each sitting, your progress will rapidly unfold before your eyes. Even when you are tired, dedicate the time for the next several weeks and magic will happen!

The first thing that I'd like you to do, assuming you haven't already, go back to what you wrote yesterday and re-read it. Do not change a thing, not even a spelling error or incomplete sentence. Just read it. Do that now, and then immediately come back to reading the remainder of this chapter for your daily exercise.

Reading Break
(Read what you wrote yesterday)

How was it? Was it exciting to read what you read? Did you want to read it to someone? I remember my first chapter and how exciting it was. I just wanted to read it to everyone. Each time you write, it is important to re-read what you wrote the previous day. It doesn't take long, and it will bring you back to where you left off. This will also help you to find gaps in your writing that you can fill in. Although I asked you not to correct any mistakes that you found for the sake of keeping you on track at the moment, you will actually correct mistakes as you review the previous day's work each day for the duration of this project.

I've explained to you about excuses and procrastination. Before you begin to write today, let me briefly give you an understanding of why people can have a tendency to procrastinate. This will help you to gain insight into why procrastination is natural, but something that you can tackle.

Our bodies are wired to heal and to return to a state of wholeness. We are wired for self-protection. When the hair stands up on the back of your neck in a bad situation, or when you don't want to get up early to get the workout that you promised yourself that you were going to get up and do, this is the body's way of keeping you safe. Whether it's personal safety or any discomfort, your body has a self-correct mechanism. This is not to say that a workout is bad, but if it causes discomfort, your brain does not know the difference between dangerous and simply uncomfortable. Your protection mechanism does have an override switch, but you have to consciously know when it has been triggered and when to flip the switch.

To flip your override switch, and this is anytime you know that you should do something that you might not want to do or simply have some sort of resistance buried, you need to quickly count from 5 backwards, out loud, and then spring into action. This audible countdown will engage your frontal cortex, coupled with the physical movement, will override procrastination. When you can't muster the creativity, or when you just don't feel like writing, immediately say 5, 4, 3, 2, 1… and get to work. Now, 5, 4, 3, 2, 1…. Let's get writing Day 5!

Your First Milestone

Today you will finish Chapter 1. Pretty unbelievable, but true. As you expand on your Day 4 writing, developing content and finalizing Chapter 1, think about how what you have introduced in Chapter 1 will tie into the rest of the book. In other words, what is the point of your writing? Are you teaching? Are you entertaining? Are you trying to evoke an action or reaction? Do a bit of planning in your mind and then journal on how the subject matter will relate to other chapters and how it will culminate in the end.

Some chapters are intended to build information from chapter to chapter, whereas others are separate stories that intermix throughout the book, and some, like cookbooks or how to guides, might have thematic sections. How you organize and link your chapters is up to you, just keep in mind, as you are developing Chapter 1, how its content relates to the big picture and how cohesive everything comes together in the end.

Today, your homework is to complete Chapter 1. Write at a minimum 1,500 words so that ideally your chapter will end somewhere in the range of no less than 3,000 words. If it's far more, that's great! The conclusion of Chapter 1 should be a culmination of all of the thoughts that you initially outlined on your index cards. If you left something out because it didn't quite fit, is this something that would be better placed in another stack of index cards to use in another chapter?

When you finish writing, take a moment to relish in your achievement. You will likely be tempted to rush ahead and move into Chapter 2. Avoid this temptation. Instead, take these ideas and note them on your index cards or take the time to journal.

If you feel especially energized at the end of Day 5 (totally normal), do some proof-reading and light editing. The more you do now, the more time you save later. You can share this with a loved one or friend by reading your work aloud to them and getting their feedback. Reading aloud will also help you find grammar mistakes that you may not find through spellcheck or by reading on your computer screen.

This excitement will carry through to tomorrow's writing experience. We will chat more on Day 6. Happy writing!

DAY 6

A Look Back at Chapter 1

Every success is usually an admission ticket to a new set of decisions.
– Henry Kissinger

You are 24 days away, just over three weeks, from being a published author. You have now written a full chapter. The process for the remaining chapters is much like the first few days:

> ➢ Arrange you're your index cards

> ➢ Read the prior day's work

> ➢ 5, 4, 3, 2, 1

> ➢ Write 1,500 words at a minimum

This will be the process that you will follow each day. That known, you have no reason to fear what, prior to now, was unknown. You completed Chapter 1 following this process. You have applied the process and know how to do it. The more you put the process into practice, the easier it gets. That does not mean that challenges won't exist, but I am going to help you overcome these as they arise from day to day.

Chapter 2 is an exciting chapter to write. Following the re-read of your Day 5 work, immediately begin on Chapter 2. This may be one of the easiest chapters for you to write because of the level of excitement over your accomplishment. This will also likely be the most notated chapter on your index cards. Something that will help you in future chapters is to understand that as ideas pop into your head as you are writing any chapter, and the idea does not fit, identify which chapters the ideas may be a better fit. Note these ideas as they pop up on your cards for the appropriate chapters and keep writing.

Strive for a larger word count today. During this entire book-writing process, each day you will have a minimum word count of 1,500 words, but if you happen to double that, more power to you. Remember, you will consistently write a minimum of 1,500 words, regardless of your word count the day before. There are no hall-passes during this 30-day period.

Now, let's take the excitement that you have from completing your first chapter and let's get writing. Happy writing. 5-4-3-2-1…Start!

DAY 7

"If you want to be successful, prepare to be doubted and tested."

Welcome to Day 7. You are now one week into your book and have a chapter and a half written. Pretty impressive, right? You have likely been able to overcome any time blockers or distractors because you only have the past six days under your belt. I will need you to remain vigilant in guarding your time and also against your mind trying to *save* you from discomfort.

They say, "diets don't fail, people fail their diets". Why is that? For anything that you desire to change, whether it is going to the gym, getting up early, or stopping smoking, we are one choice away from derailment. Our ego desires feeling good and anytime you contradict the *feel-good* sensation and introduce something that will potentially feel less uncomfortable, the ego tries to self-correct. This is when you may begin to make up excuses like, "I really don't feel like getting up early, I will go to the gym later." Or, "I just don't feel motivated to write, I will write double tomorrow."

WARNING! You are one decision away from derailment. Do not accept that you don't feel motivated, you are too busy, or you can't think of what to write about. Any excuse to skip a daily writing session can be overcome with 5, 4, 3, 2, 1... start. You must manually, consciously override these thoughts. Once you are sitting down writing, your goal is to complete the task. Each day this can be one of the most satisfying tasks of the day. The next three weeks are an easy win for you. At the end, the goal is for you to publish your book. Limiting thoughts will not get you there, a purposive decision to just do it will.

Don't Count on Your Memory

Let's reflect on where you are in the process. You have written a chapter and a half. Today you will complete Chapter 2 or one-fifth of your book. How is your writing developing and how are your thoughts unfolding? Are you thinking of additional items, either when you are away from your book or while you are writing, and capturing those thoughts on your index cards and your thoughts or feelings about the process in your journal? As I explained, I have lost, or at least not remembered in their fullness far too many ideas as they originally came to me, when I failed to write down my thoughts immediately. For this reason, the voice recorder on your phone may be an ideal backup system to ensure you never lose anything.

I used to commute to and from work an hour and a half to two hours per day. During this time, I would often have quotes come to me for a blog or a new concept to introduce in one of my books. I began using the audio recording tool on my iPhone to record memos while driving. By doing so, I was able to transfer these memos to my cards or directly to my blog later. I was able to keep the integrity of the original thought by capturing it in this manner. This has been a valuable tool. Most recently I do voice notes in my phone's notepad. I simply hit the microphone and the phone transcribes what I say. It is really handy to open up my notepad when I sit down to write as I have the ideas right there in front of me. The point is, no matter how earth-shattering the thought is, you risk losing it in the craziness of daily life if you do not put in place a way to immediately capture all ideas as they emerge.

Over the next several weeks, thoughts of your book will, and should, consume you. It will be very natural for thoughts to come while you are dreaming, falling asleep, at work, in a conversation with someone, or while in the shower. Get in the habit of capturing thoughts and providing yourself with convenient ways to capture them as they come.

Success Tip: If you are not writing directly onto an index card, make sure that you begin your next writing session by adding your new notes to the appropriate chapter and card.

Alright, now that you have tips and tricks to ensure your success, it's time to re-read yesterday's work and get started. Tomorrow you begin Chapter 3, so your task today is to bring the second half of Chapter 2 to life and conclude it so that your reader has a reason to look forward to Chapter 3.

The key to any literary piece, regardless of whether it is fiction or non-fiction is to have the reader look forward to the next chapter. When a chapter ends, the reader is provided an opportunity to pause for the moment, or resume. Give your readers an opportunity for choice. You can introduce an idea, thought, concept, twist, or story which resumes in the next chapter or you can complete the thought, concept or story. In fiction this means that you might leave the reader hanging. In non-fiction this means that you may summarize the points of the chapter or briefly hint at how the topic of the next chapter will help the reader.

Whichever approach you take to conclude your chapter, give the reader a reason to continue reading. Think about your conclusion to lure your leader forward as you are wrapping up your chapter. What will make your reader want to continue on to the next chapter? What will make the reader turn the page?

It's time to begin. Happy completion of week one. Remember why you are doing this. Reflect often. Embrace the journey.

When you change the way you look at things,
the things you look at change.

DAY 8

Don't expect to see a change if you don't make one.

Welcome to week two of your book-writing. It's time to journal. Answer the following question: What has been your greatest challenge this past week?

For many, daily life disruptions can be the greatest challenge. We have so many responsibilities and it may feel like writing seems like a selfish pleasure as you carve out time to write. This is simply your ego squawking. There is nothing selfish about you achieving your dream. Again, this is a self-defense mechanism to protect you from disappointment, which ironically is rooted in a belief that you can't do it. You can and you are worth investing time into and your dreams are worth investing in.

As for life, *life happens*, believe me, I totally get that. Your dream of writing a book will soon be a reality, regardless of how much *life happens*. It may even help you get through other disappointments in your life as it is a great distractor. Wouldn't you rather be distracted by succeeding at your dream than anything else? This healthy distraction helps you to shift your mindset to one that is better positioned to face the world. A *can-do* mindset is the result of feeling that you are succeeding at a goal. By following through on your daily writing habits, you are taking action to ensure your goal achievement. You may soon have people making comments like, "There is something different about you". It's success. Wear it proudly.

Before we get started writing today, I wanted to explain the difference between self-publishing and traditional publishing. Self-publishing means that your book is 100% yours. You absorb the costs for publishing, printing, promoting, and distributing, but you also maintain 100% of the profits.

In traditional publishing, your work is represented. The publishing company is like a broker and marketer for your work. The publisher typically, with exception, takes on the costs to print, market, and distribute your book. Traditional publishers want your book to be successful because they have a financial motive. They make money when you make money. The more you make, the more they make. I should probably clarify that it's truly the other way around because your share is far less than the publisher's share. This is the cost of business.

There are some hybrid publishing houses that will charge you for the printing and other associated costs in exchange for publishing under their imprint and visibility through their marketing channels. Prices can be rather steep ($5,000-$15,000 or more) and this type of publishing, regardless of the company imprint, will not guarantee higher book sales. You will still need to be promoting and marketing your work.

Choosing a self-published route does not mean that your work will go unnoticed. There have been some huge self-published success stories. What self-publishing does mean, especially for your first work, is a sense of completion and accomplishment, and that your royalties are not linked to an advance of anticipated sales. In other words, you make more money on each book and you own the rights.

I will give you details in future chapters on the steps involved in seeking a publisher, so that if you choose, in the future to seek traditional publishing, you will understand the process. For now, let's focus on strategies for your daily writing. You have just three weeks left in the process and as I stated earlier, life happens. What we want to make sure is that you use life's distractions to amplify your commitment. Nothing will get in your way.

Today you are beginning Chapter 3. This is an important Chapter, as it is, what I like to call, a *developing chapter*. This is a ten-chapter book so somewhere between Chapter 3 and 4, the book is about one-third completed. I like to arrange my cards before I begin Chapter 3 and look for themes. If I were to group two to four chapters together in three main groups, what would that look like?

Chapter 3 often is the chapter where ideas or characters that have been introduced are expanded upon to build the story or used to examine linkage to other concepts. Chapter 3 helps to develop richness of your book. I don't want you to feel additional pressure wherein you think that Chapter 3 needs to be the most sensational chapter, instead I want you think of Chapter 3 as a culmination of the preceding two chapters as you enhance what has been said. Chapter 3 is your opportunity to start weaving the story or concepts together.

Let's get started. 5, 4, 3, 2, 1... See you on Day 9.

DAY 9

Some people dream of success, while other people get up every morning and make it happen. – Wayne Huizenga

Happy Day 9! It is pretty incredible to think that today you will have completed three full chapters of your book. That means in just 14 days, your writing will be completed. This does not mean that you will be done, as we will have a few items to attend to for publishing once your writing is completed. For now, however, you have a solid start on your book. You are roughly one-third through writing your book and hopefully it has been enjoyable.

Before we get started today I'd like you to take a moment to reinforce your commitment to yourself. I cannot tell you how many people, as I began talking about this book, told me, "I need that book." Why is that? Why is it that so many people desire to write, yet don't? For exactly the same reason as you and I experienced— they don't know where to begin. Now that you have three chapters under your belt, do you wonder why you didn't start this sooner? Does it seem surreal that in just two more weeks your book will be written? Do you even believe it? It's okay if you have doubt, but we need to help you believe in yourself, your commitment, and your dream.

Writing a book is something that many desire and few achieve. It has become a joke within both academic and speaker communities when someone says that they are writing a book. Everyone seems to be *working* on a book, but nobody seems to be finishing. Why is that?

Again, it is because fear and doubt are debilitating. When we don't have a clear picture of where we are going, no matter how strongly we desire what we want, achieving our desire is much more difficult. It's just as Zig Ziglar once said, "If you aim at nothing, you will hit it every time."

Perseverance – It's So Very Worth It

What I have provided for you is a plan to visualize the writing process. Although we aren't getting into what happens after the writing process yet, you know that if you follow specific steps for 20 days that you will have your 10 book chapters written. That's pretty remarkable. So instead of "I'm *working* on a book." You are actually completing your book. To accomplish this, a daily commitment for 30 days is required.

During my year one residency for my doctoral program, we were informed that only 1% of those that enter the program finish. 1%! That is staggering! During my entire doctoral program, when I would get tired, frustrated, or just not feel like working on my dissertation, I would remind myself of my commitment of becoming one of the 1%-club. Consider yourself as a published author in this same group. I suspect that for all the people that say they want to write a book or even those that say they are working on a book, that it is far less than 1% that actually finish.

Success Tip: Your daily commitment and determination to sticking the course, for just 30 days, will result in your achievement, fulfillment, and sense of accomplishment. As you get ready to complete Chapter 3 today, evaluate any challenges that you may have encountered over your past few days writing. I suggest that you write down any of these challenges in your journal and next to these items note anything that you might do to eliminate these challenges. These can become additional daily habits. If you cannot completely eliminate them, how can you lessen them? Secondly, write down any of the things that have gone really well. For each item that you have noted as going well, how can you use this to make your writing experience more enjoyable each day? These serve as reinforcements to your success. The completed list of challenges and things that went well is your success recipe. Use this recipe as a daily reminder when you feel stuck and help get you back on the right path. Learn from what didn't go so well by creating new daily habits and do more of what went well to enhance your writing experience.

Today your task is to complete Chapter 3. Once you are done, I'd like you to re-read Chapters 1-3. After you are done reading, look at the cards for your remaining chapters. Did something come to mind that you need to add? If so, please add any notes to your cards. Did you have any additional insights from your reading such as groups of people who might be interested in your book or ideas of how to spread the word about your book? Break out your journal and jot down your insights.

Alright, let's get started. It's time to finish Chapter 3.

5, 4, 3, 2, 1....

DAY 10

The difference between a successful person and others is not a lack of strength, not a lack of knowledge, but rather a lack in will. – Vince Lombardi

Welcome to Day 10. Since you re-read Chapters 1-3 yesterday, you will not be re-reading yesterday's work. What you will be doing in place of that is to ensure that you have your index cards grouped not only by chapter, but also all 10 chapters should also be grouped into three distinct categories. In fiction you might consider the following groups types: 1) Plot/Foundation/Background, 2) Introduction of problem, and 3) Problem climax/resolution. In non-fiction you might consider the following groupings: 1) Background/Foundational Concepts, 2) Actions/Application 3) Reinforcement/Take-Aways.

When you arrange your card groups by major categories it will help you to maintain focus on the purpose of the part of the book you are working on. Chances are Chapter 3 will be the final chapter for your first category. It's perfectly okay to have imbalance of groups of cards in the categories. For example, you may find that your plot category only needs two chapters to lay out the story line and introduce characters, or maybe you need four or five chapters in that category. There is no hard and fast rule, but typically you will identify three to four common themes for assigning categories.

Now what? Once you have grouped your cards into categories, is there something that you might have mentioned in the first three chapters that you did not? If so, when we begin writing today, go back and fill in any gaps in the story. Gap filling activities are not counted in your daily word count, you still have a 1,500 word minimum writing assignment for today.

Assuming Chapter 3 wrapped up the first thematic category, Chapter 4 will begin with the second theme in mind. Think of these categories like a sandwich. Categories 1 and 3 are like the bread. These categories sandwich the *meat* of the book. What happens if you have a sandwich with holes in one of the pieces of bread? You risk items in the middle falling out. At the very least, it's very difficult to manage. Categories will help you hold it all together and help you make sense of the ingredients.

Once you are happy with your categories, we are going to get to work on today's writing task. You have already re-read your chapters, so you are in the perfect place to shape the second category. Adding *meat* to your book is you adding substance and richness. The middle chapters are where you will shine. Think about the purpose of your writing. Do you want to share a story on the power of love? Would you like to help someone gain the knowledge that they need to get to where they want to be? Think about your purpose for the fiction or non-fiction book that you are writing. Group two is where your purpose will become evident. Begin with this thought in mind—

I am telling this story to accomplish … (fill in the blank).

Think of the significance of the foundation that you laid in the first three chapters to this next category. You laid the groundwork, now add substance. 1,500 words minimum is your homework.

5, 4, 3, 2, 1…

Day 11

If you don't sacrifice for what you want, what you want becomes the sacrifice.

Today I'd like to continue the conversation that I began a few days ago on the difference between self-publishing and traditional publishing. I'd like to focus on traditional publishing. Seeking a publisher is a multi-step process and although this book is not intended for those seeking traditional publishing, understanding what is needed to seek a publisher is important. A step that you have completed, although in a much looser format, that is required for a book proposal to a publisher is a book outline.

A book proposal to a prospective publisher includes a detailed outline. Although you don't need a book proposal in self-publishing because you are the publisher, the outline is very important, and much of what I am about to explain is similar to what you have completed up through your Day 10 assignment, with the exception of Step 4.

Step 1: Develop chapter titles

Step 2: Develop main points for each chapter

Step 3: Categorize your chapters into themes

Step 4: Write a synopsis for each theme.

The following is what a book proposal on becoming a pet parent might look like. Within each of the parts below are summarized data from several chapters. For example, Part I may include Chapter 1, 2, and 3.

Part I. The Responsibility of a Pet Owner

Here you would provide a brief summary (synopsis) of how these chapters would support this topic. You will have no less than 3 or 4 sentences in your summary.

Part II. The Proper Care and Feeding of Pets

Summarize the main points that are covered in the chapters that make up this group of chapters.

Part III. Pet Obedience

Summarize the main points that are covered in the chapters that make up this group of chapters.

Part IV. Lifetime through the Golden Years

Summarize the main points that are covered in the chapters that make up this group of chapters.

The second step of this process is to write a second outline that includes a 3-4 sentence summary of each chapter. Even though you haven't written these chapters, you already know what you are going to write about in these chapters because of your talking points. Use your talking points to develop this summary. Your outline should look something like the example that follows.

Introduction

Introduce the premise of your book and who would want to read it and what they would gain by doing so. No more than one paragraph.

Part I. The Responsibility of a Pet Owner

Chapter 1: Title. Summary in one paragraph.

Chapter 2: Title. Summary in one paragraph.

Chapter 3: Title. Summary in one paragraph.

Part II. The Proper Care and Feeding of Pets

Chapter 4: Title. Summary in one paragraph.

Chapter 5: Title. Summary in one paragraph.

Part III. Pet Obedience

Chapter 6: Title. Summary in one paragraph.

Chapter 7: Title. Summary in one paragraph.

Chapter 8: Title. Summary in one paragraph.

Part IV. Lifetime through the Golden Years

Chapter 9: Title. Summary in one paragraph.

Chapter 10: Title. Summary in one paragraph.

Like I explained previously, although you are not seeking a publishing house, at least for now it's always good to understand the process. The outline is a major piece of the book proposal and also as you will discover, a major piece of your self-publishing effort.

There are many things that are roughly the same if you are self-publishing or seeking a publisher. In future days, I will expand on the book proposal, but for today I wanted you to understand that your efforts, up to this point, are very similar regardless of the publishing route you choose. Keep in mind that I'm not just giving you tasks as busy work. Each task serves a strategic purpose in the culmination of your project.

Now that we have established some significance and importance to the efforts that you have undertaken thus far, let's use that feeling of empowerment to launch today's writing effort. You have much to be proud of as you enter into the *meat* of your book. Give your readers something to chew on. Happy writing.

DAY 12

Work hard in silence, let your success be your noise. – Frank Ocean

Welcome to the half-way point of your book. Today you will be beginning Chapter 5. Up until now, your focus each day has been following a ritual of steps:

1) review the prior day's writing;

2) review your index cards;

3) write a minimum of 1,500 words.

Throughout each day as you think of new ideas, you have been noting those ideas on the index cards for the chapter for which they are associated and journaling insights. Today, I'd like you to start thinking of your final product. Each day I am going to give you a new assignment that will help prepare you for readying your book for publication.

On Day 1 you were asked a few questions. One of those questions was to visualize your book. Today, your task is to think about the cover of your book. How do you envision your cover? Is there a picture? A solid background? What color is it? What about the title of your book? What is the title? What color is the font? Cover design is important, and you may have absolutely no clue about how to design a cover. That's okay.

Search Amazon, Barnes & Noble, or another online retailer of books website. Look at the book covers throughout these websites. What catches your eye? Make yourself some notes or save pictures of the covers that you like. Why do you like a particular cover style?

Your book cover can be designed in a basic template or can be customized. A cover design does not need to cost much, if anything. There are some very affordable, as well as free, cover design options. If you are semi-design literate you can use Canva.com book templates to design both the front and the back of your book. I would highly recommend that if you cannot use Photoshop and do not want a stock template cover design that you investigate Fiverr.com. Fiverr is a freelance marketplace for just about anything that you may need for your book. I absolutely love Fiverr to develop marketing materials, editing, and cover design work. I've had covers designed with prices ranging from $89-469 on Fiverr. I now have designers that I use regularly through this freelance site.

Once you decide on a design style for your cover, put together a file of what you like. Make a list of book cover designers available on Fiverr. Most have base pricing available without contacting the freelancer for a quote. Make a list of the artists that you may want to work with that are within your price range. Do not assume that the least expensive will produce shoddy work. I have had some amazing results from Fiverr at all price points.

You will be coming back to your cover design file in another week, but I'd like you to keep this handy. You will be using this file over the week as you gather additional information on the self-publishing process. The more you prepare as we go along, the simpler the process in another week.

Today, you are beginning Chapter 5. Keep in mind that if you still have no clue what you would like on the cover of your book at this point, as you write, a character or an idea from your writing may inspire you. This happened to me during Chapter 4 of my last book. The cover became evident as I wrote the chapter and it served as an inspiration as I completed the book.

As you begin the mid-point of your book, remaining inspired and motivated is critical. You have now been working on your book for nearly two weeks and today you will be exactly half way done. Let your progress inspire you. Had you not started 12 days ago, you would still be one of those that has *always wanted to write a book*. Instead, you are almost done with your book. Harness that excitement. Use the excitement today as you write. Push yourself. Now get writing.

DAY 13

Don't just stand there; make something happen. – Lee Iacocca

Staying motivated during your 30-day book writing period is essential to your success. It's incredibly easy to come up with excuses to put off your daily writing exercises to the next day. I urge you not to give in to this temptation. Experts suggest that tracking one's progress may serve as a successful motivation technique. The reason for this is that wherever you invest your time and energy is where you will reap the benefits. Reminding yourself of your progress toward achieving what you want helps you to visualize reaching your goal.

Another way to stay motivated is to write from a place of passion. Before you begin writing each day, remind yourself why you wanted to write the book in the first place. This will translate into your writing and help motivate you in the same way a smile can be sensed by a listener over the phone. Your passion will be conveyed through your writing. Everything is energy and energy is everything. Let the energy of your passion flow through you and serve as a catalyst to accomplish your daily habits.

Finally, affirmation and positivity are two of the most critical success factors to help keep you motivated. As you share your progress with others and talk about how great you feel about your progress and the project, make notes of positive comments that others say to you. I like to put these on post-its and post them around my writing space, on the bathroom mirror, or around the house.

You will undoubtedly come across dream crushers that will give you advice that they will assure you *is just to protect you from being hurt.* This type of advice isn't worth holding onto or getting flustered over as this won't serve your motivation. It's useless. Take note of positive advice, support and comments. Feed your soul with what you need to push yourself. Physically writing down positivity will serve as your affirmation. State these affirmations as *"I" statements.* For example, someone says, "This is great. I'm so proud of you." You read the statement. "I am doing something great. I am so proud of myself."

The more positivity and affirmation that you surround yourself with the better. Note your progress, write from a place of passion, record positive comments, and state affirmations of everything positive from these motivation tools. As you complete this book, applying these motivation techniques will help you through Day 30 when you complete the process.

Today you will complete writing Chapter 5. What an accomplishment! Remember to refocus before your review and writing exercises today. You have peaked the mountain that you sought to climb, and you are on your way to the victory line. Happy writing!

DAY 14

Don't stop when you're tired. Stop when you are done.

On Day 12, you put some thought into your cover design. Today, I'd like you to consider the back cover. Often the back cover of a book will contain endorsements from others, such as celebrities, academics, or book reviewers. The back may also provide a teaser, a bit about the plot and a riveting quote. Finally, the author's picture and a bit about the author might be found on the back of the book.

This is the time to put some thought into the content for the back cover. If you are interested in endorsements, seek them from friends and colleagues that are affiliated with universities, well-known businesses, or organizations that align with the content of your writing. For example, if you are writing a book on Interview Tips and Techniques, you may want to seek out an HR Director, career coach, or CEO that either you know personally, or that a friend or acquaintance may know. Be ready to provide this person with a proofread version of your first three chapters.

Ask your potential endorsers for just a sentence or two to help you promote your book. Let them know that you will provide them with a free copy of the book as soon as it is published. Always show your appreciation to those who are willing to help you along the way. You can never go wrong being appreciative and gracious.

I'd like you to jot down some notes about the back cover of your book. What do you want on the back cover? Again, you can visit

Amazon.com or go to the bookstore or library to check out the back covers of an assortment of books. Add these notes to your cover design folder. Keep in mind that if you want to use a headshot of yourself that the file will need to be 300 dpi sized. You may want to enlist the help of a friend or family member that is into photography or graphics.

If you or someone else does your book cover, you will need to have everything ready. Cover elements can sneak up on you if you don't put the work in now. You need content for the back, just as you need content inside the book. Start compiling the pieces so that later you can just pull them out of your file. I put together the following:

- Testimonials
- Enticing Synopsis
- Author Photo
- Author Short Bio (I put a longer version inside the book)
- ISBN (we will cover this soon)
- Barcode (we will cover this as well)

Getting Over the Hump

You have five chapters completed and five more to go. How is the writing coming along? What have your biggest challenges been thus far? Stop and take a moment to think of just two things that you could do to eliminate or reduce those challenges. Choose to initiate just one of those two things today. What will your habit be to minimize your challenge?

Before you re-read your writing from yesterday, I'd like you to spread out your cards for Chapters 6-10. Now that you have been writing for over a week, you have likely found that when you are re-reading your work from the day before that you find areas that you could expand upon. Today, I'd like you to look at your cards to identify potential missed points. You have developed five chapters so far which likely has spurred additional points that you may want to cover. You are beginning to get the hang of this writing thing so identifying gaps within your writing when it is still in the form of cards is essential.

Once you are done reviewing and adding points to your cards, you can move on to re-reading your work from yesterday. As you read, I'd like you examine how thoroughly you explain a point or concept or how you elaborate elements of the story. This is an area that many writers could improve. Just because it seems clear as day within your thoughts doesn't mean that you will always do it justice on paper. Look for gaps or areas that need elaboration and add what is needed.

Chapter 6 is a milestone chapter. You are past the half way point and working your way to the finish line. Savor the writing experience. Don't write just to hit your word quota for the day. Write because you have a great story or knowledge to share. Before you know it, you will be putting the period at the last line of your final chapter. You know the drill. 5, 4, 3, 2, 1…

DAY 15

Success is not accident. It is hard work, perseverance, learning, studying, sacrifice, and most of all, love of what you are doing – Pele

Welcome to Day 15. Yesterday I had you identify the greatest challenges that you have experienced thus far in writing your book. I asked you to implement one thing that could help reduce a challenge that you have experienced. It is my hope that whatever challenges you identified that today you made a concerted effort to initiate one change to eliminate that road block. Each day, starting today, I'd like you to reflect on the two challenges that you have identified and how they inhibit your productivity or writing or how you have overcome one or all of them. Your task is to journal how your change(s) in daily habits are impacting your writing today. Your journal entry might look something like this.

When I get home from work, I'm tired and I don't really want to get right into writing. I know that if I start writing too late, I may not be able to concentrate because that has happened. By giving myself 30 minutes to unwind when I get home, I feel refreshed and ready to dive into my writing. This has helped me stay on track.

Over the next five days, before you start your daily writing, I'd like you to write a few thoughts in your notebook or journal as to how making this one change has helped. I want you to only focus on the positive. Even if the change made a minuscule impact, I'd like you to pay this homage by acknowledging it's impact. Maybe you set your alarm clock 15 minutes earlier.

Although the change in my daily schedule only bought me fifteen more minutes to devote to my writing, I have fifteen minutes more than I had before the change.

What this activity is designed to do is shift tracks in your thinking. It's easy to see little change as failure, but instead, when we see these as successes, regardless how slight, it's natural to continue moving in the same direction. By introducing a thought about the positive benefit that you have experienced from one small change, you will automatically start seeking ways to improve even more. Small changes equal big results.

You Want to Read My Book!

Today you will be finishing Chapter 6. With just four more chapters to go, I'd like you to think about how you want to spread the news about your book. Just because your book is available on a major website does not guarantee anyone will find it on their own without being guided to it. You will need a marketing plan.

But you don't need to have a degree in Marketing to market your book. There are many ways to market your book, however you are going to need to put a plan together. A few days ago, I provided you with a portion of information on the book proposal process to a traditional publisher. A major component of the book proposal is your marketing plan.

Publishers want to know what type of audience you already have and how you are going to promote your work. Like I said, just because you write it, there is no guarantee that you will have any buyers or readers. You have to give people a reason to want to buy and read your book. If they don't know your book even exists, how will you tell them?

Think about the last library or large bookstore that you were in. Think about the volumes and volumes of books by authors that you have never heard of and book titles you never knew existed. This is no way means that the author failed in any way. There are just too many books in the world for you to be intimately aware of every author and book in existence. That is why it is critical for you to put a plan together to market your work.

Social media has made book promotion to friends, family, and the world easier than ever, but you have much noise to compete with. Everyone has a message. "Notice me." How will you make your message memorable? I suggest signing up as an author on Goodreads so that you will have a forum as an author that you can drive people from your other social media sites to for book giveaways, discussions, and so forth. You can use your Facebook, Twitter, or other social media contacts as "please help spread the word network." Keep in mind, what's in it for me?

What value are you adding when you are asking people to share? What are they getting in return? Maybe you can offer that anyone who shares your book marketing piece on social media and receives 100 likes, you will give them a free copy of your book or maybe enter them in a special drawing for your book. Maybe you offer them access to exclusive content. Think about what you can offer. The more you give, the more you receive. I'm always dreaming up freebies to engage my audience and potential audience. Who doesn't like a freebie?

Where else can you spread the word for your book? Everywhere! Mom and Pop bookstores might be interested in you coming and doing a reading and signing copies of your book for a percentage of sales. Two of my favorite places to do author signings are Half Price Books and Barnes and Nobel. They are amazing at providing in store author opportunities, which typically includes flyers at the counters and posters on the doors in advance of the event and promotion on their websites.

Start putting a list together of ways that you are going to get the word out on your book. The ways to market your work are limitless. Start with the easy ones, like a book launch party at church or with a club you are a member of, a reading at the public library, and even posting flyers on bulletin boards. Get creative and have fun thinking of new ways to spread the news. Now go finish Chapter 6.

DAY 16

Great things never came from comfort zones.

It's pretty wild to think of the fact that you are starting Chapter 7, but it just goes to show you that with a bit of guidance, a plan, and a whole lot of commitment, you can achieve anything that you set your mind to. Once you get into the habit of writing, it gets much easier to start and harder to stop. When I'm on a roll, I don't want to stop.

Writing and publishing your book isn't all about writing. You have much to do to prepare your book for publication. Today, your focus is on editing. The sooner you get to it, the better. Beginning no later than Day 20, you will need to know how you are going to edit your book. Do you have a friend or family member that was an English major in college? Maybe you know a retired school teacher, or your children are still in school and you can ask around. Teachers and retired teachers make great editors. Again, you can find an editor on Fiverr.com. My suggestion is by Day 20 that you have someone beginning your edit on the chapters that you have completed.

A word of caution about the edit process. You need to get your ego out of the way to achieve the best results. When you editor suggests changes, avoid getting defensive. Your goal is to have a polished document that flows well and is free of grammatical and punctuation errors. Let this person do their job and take their advice. They are helping you. Once you get back the first heavily red-lined edit from your editor, you will thank me for warning you. It's okay to feel yourself getting defensive. It's normal. This is your baby that they are critiquing and tearing apart. Get over it. Accept the input and integrate changes and move on. We need to get you to the finish line.

If you are using a website like Fiverr.com to find an editor, keep in mind what the freelancer's turnaround time is for the price. To keep on track, you will need to start feeding an editor complete chapters. Most editors can turn around a single chapter in 24-48 hours. Keep in mind that you cannot wait until Day 29 to send your chapters out to edit. Day 20 is your deadline to start your editing and ideally you will have your entire book edited by Day 23.

Today, as you start Chapter 7, keep in mind that this should be the third section of chapters in your book. Chapter 7 should be where you begin to present the final elements. In fiction, this is usually where the plot thickens to wind the story through the concluding chapters. For non-fiction, such as self-help, Chapter 7 is the beginning of the culmination of concepts and advise on the application of these concepts for improvement.

As you review yesterday's writing think of how to begin Chapter 7 in a way that provides distinction of the shift from one section to the next. Think of your book as Section 1: Intro, Section 2: Body, and Section 3: Conclusion. How will you begin to tie together everything that you have written thus far? Put some thought into how you are going to hold your reader's attention until the very last line of the book. Enjoy your writing. You are so close! 5, 4, 3, 2, 1…

DAY 17

Successful and unsuccessful people do not vary greatly in their abilities. They vary in their desires to reach their potential. – John Maxwell

On Day 1, I had you write down and answer several questions. One of those questions was "Who would be interested in your book and why?" As I have explained the book proposal process, pitching your book to a prospective publisher or agent has many pieces. The marketing piece, how you promote your work includes an integral piece that must be identified. Who is your audience?

You can promote your book on Twitter and Facebook all day but if you don't target the audience that your writing would appeal to, your efforts will likely not yield the fruit that you would like. 'Who is your audience?' is not as easy a question as you might think. 'Everybody' is not the answer either. Seriously, everybody would be super cool, but really there is an ideal group of people that would be interested in your book—you need to figure out who that group is. Are they kids, adults, married, empty-nesters, outdoorsy, adventurers, into science-fiction, or romance?

Determining who your book will appeal to is a big deal because until you know who would be interested, it's pretty tough to know how to reach those folks. In your writing journal, expand on the answer that you provided on Day 1. Think on paper. Make a list of the various groups or individuals that you believe would connect with your book.

Next, make a list of how you might target market to these groups.

Although this book is intended for those who will self-publish, the book proposal information that you would use to pitch to someone else is exactly the information that you will need to promote your work yourself. Each element of the book proposal is a piece of your success recipe.

An exercise that may help you to identify your audience is to review each chapter and make a list of something that you like from each chapter and why it would be meaningful, enjoyable, or relevant to your reader. Would they be inspired? Would it give them hope? Would they feel led on an adventure or into suspense? Take note of whatever the impact that you believe your writing might have on people. Who would and how would readers be impacted? For example, if you noted that in each chapter of your self-help weight-loss book that people would be given hope, why? *People who have struggled to lose weight on one diet after another, only to gain it back again, will find this one small change could make all the difference in the world for finally achieving lasting results.*

You've determine in your chapter review that concepts of your book speak to people who have been stuck in a yo-yo diet, giving them hope to finally break the cycle. What does that group look like? Are they older or of all age groups? How might you market to that group? Where do you find people interested in permanent weight loss?

Take some time over the next 24 hours to really put some thought into who your book will appeal to and how you will reach those people groups. A bit of thought and planning now will pay off later.

Inspired Writing

Now to the good stuff. Yesterday you began Chapter 7 and today you will finish Chapter 7. Hopefully your index cards have been sufficiently detailed for each chapter so that you have plenty of points to draw from. If you have been struggling for word count each day, use visualization to spark your innovation and creativity. Sometimes words get hung up and they just need a jiggle to free them.

Close your eyes and allow yourself to daydream about this chapter. Fiction is suited exceptionally well for visualization because you can imagine your characters interacting. Surprisingly, non-fiction, especially self-help, can be really fun to imagine. Imagine the topic of your chapter coming to life in someone's life and changing their life for the better. How would this happen? What does it look like? If you are writing on how to find your dream job, imagine what the person who lands their dream job looks like. What concept in the chapter did they put into practice? What did that look like as they were doing it? What obstacles might they encounter? Think about how you will speak to that by answering these questions. The more you see, the more you can describe. The more substance and details that you provide in your writing, the better reader experience as it will be a more enriching reading journey.

Today as you begin to write, visualize your writing as it is playing out in front of you. Are you missing a step? Be thorough and provide rich descriptions so that others can develop a vision. You are the artist.

Get Ready

For tomorrow's activities you will need blank index cards.

DAY 18

By Chapter 8 you have had to have felt stuck at some point on either word count or writing at length on various of your index card points. Don't feel alone. Remember, I'm writing this with you and I get stuck too. I'm sure that this writing project is not the only time that you have felt stuck. It's natural to feel stuck from time to time, whether it's picking a paint color for your living room or while working on a big project at the office. There are some strategies, however, that you can employ to help get unstuck.

When you find yourself stuck, do a system re-boot. Just like when your computer freezes up and you need to do a hard shut down to get things fired up again, sometimes we need a system re-boot. Shake up your routine. Getting yourself to a state of inspiration can happen in many ways but it is not by doing the same thing that you are doing.

If you typically write at the end of the day after a long day at work or dealing with the kids, try waking up early for your writing exercise. Better yet, try physically stimulating inspiration. You would be amazed how a walking, lifting weights, or hoping on the treadmill will help free your mind.

When I am stuck, I recognize that I am at the threshold of opportunity. I have an opportunity to choose to stay in the same spot or choose to do something spectacular. Remember, when we get stuck in a rut, our brain is just keeping us from discomfort by keeping us on a habitually safe path.

Imagine a narrow dirt path, well-grooved from streams of rain making its way toward the lowest point. Now imagine that you are riding your bike down that path. What happens when you get too close to the edge of the worn groove of the path? Your bike tire naturally gets pulled into the rut and you find yourself travelling into rut. Yes, you are literally in a rut. You actually have to work to get yourself out of the rut by steering your bike up the side of hill onto the path to either side.

When you get stuck in the rut, your path is determined for you, which really doesn't get you anywhere spectacular. Challenging the rut, getting unstuck by breaking away from limitations is key. What happens when you are in a writer's rut? What happens when you just stare at the computer screen? The same old path. Get away from the screen and do something completely different and preferably physical.

Neuroscientist Wendy Suzuki posits that physical stimulation through exercise may help improve memory and imagination. This is because Brain Derived Neurotrophic Factor (BDNF), which is the stimulant to brain cell growth, are stimulated through physical activity. The mind body connection when you engage yourself through exercise is astounding. The key is to focus on every aspect of the physical activity. If you decide to lift weights, really engage your mind with the feeling of the weights in your hands and the physical sensation as the muscles work. You need to engage your mind at the same time as your body. A walk around the neighborhood may do wonders as you take in details.

Pay attention to the cracks in the sidewalk, your neighbor's landscaping, paint colors on the houses, and the activities going on. Listen to the birds or the traffic while you feel the wind, warm sun, or bitter cold on your face. Immerse yourself in a physical, sensation-fest. Your mind will be absorbing in so many details that what you were stuck on will loosen up. This is because when you free yourself to stop thinking about the rut, you steer yourself out of the rut.

Now that you have some tactics for combatting the rut, I hope your last few days of writing are exceptionally satisfying. This is an exciting time for you. Today you will be not only starting Chapter 8, but you will also be developing your author biography for your "About the Author" page. This is a bit about you. An author's page, or author's bio, is typically located at the end of a book and is meant to tell readers a little about the author of the book. A good author bio is short and highlights basic professional information but may also include a bit of personal information. This is especially true for fiction writers where professional qualifications or subject matter expertise aren't relevant. The author's page is an opportunity for you, the author, to connect with your readers and provide them with insight into who you are. In the area of non-fiction, the author bio provides readers with the author's credentials. What makes you an authority on the subject matter?

I'd like you to follow the same structure for your author page bio as you used in developing your book chapters, index cards. Take out three index cards. On the first card, write your name, followed by what makes you stand out in this world. Do you make a mean cup of coffee? Are you the world's best shower singer (in your mind)? Have you devoted every summer for the past five years to helping out at the local recreation center? Silly or serious, have some fun with this but dig deep. If you can't think of anything, ask people around you what they think you are great at or what they love most about you. Write it down!

On the second card write down why you wrote your book. You only get two sentences MAXIMUM, so make it count.

Card three is something personal. This could be something along the lines of your marital status, number of children, pets, hobbies, or whatever you want to share.

The cards serve as your outline. In short, these cards serve as your what, why, and who.

Your bio should be somewhere in the range of 100-250 words. Write this in third person. Your opening should grab the attention of your readers.

Now, if the thing that you are really great at was shower singer, sorry, you aren't going to be using that, but that serves as a prompting mechanism to dig deep. I know, I'm a party pooper, but really, I'm just getting the party started. Your shower singing might prompt thinking along the line of something like this: "Jane Smith's love for telling children's stories began more than a decade ago when she volunteered at the local library. Since then, people have been singing praise for her creative and whimsical stories that transport her readers to magical lands." You can then compare your writing to what inspired your writing. "The colorful illustrations of Eric Carle served as an inspiration to Jane as she developed her own unique style."

Finally wrap up with something personal. "Jane lives on a 250-acre apple orchard in upstate New York with her husband and two children. In her spare-time she enjoys hiking in the woods."

The goal of your bio is to help your readers get to know you, **what** drives you, why you are qualified to write on the topic, or **why** you are writing at all, and **who** you are. It's pretty basic. Check out a few books that you may have on your bookshelf to get some ideas as to style.

Your bio is in addition to your writing assignment today. So with that extra bit of work added to your plate, you better get to it. Happy writing.
5,4,3,2,1…..

DAY 19

The biggest adventure you can take is to live the life of your dreams.

You don't know how tempted I am to simply instruct you to complete Chapter 8 and then I'd be done with my daily writing exercise. Yes, like you, I too struggle to find the motivation to write some days. What I like to remind myself when I commit to something is that if I put off just one day, I've robbed myself of the satisfaction of a feeling of accomplishment one day sooner. Think about this - How many times have you gone on a diet, committed to going to the gym, getting up early, or any number of self-promises, and then made the decision to go against that commitment? How did it make you feel when you eventually gave it up all together? I'd venture to guess, not so great.

Why do we do this to ourselves? Why do we sabotage what we really want? Unfortunately, we often have good intentions with wanting *a little break*, but that break can turn into a hiatus and then abandonment of our dream.

There is an incredible feeling to be experienced waiting on the other side of completion—it's called satisfaction from accomplishment. Satisfaction from accomplishment is self-love. It is a feeling like an internal self-hug. Satisfaction is confirmation to the psyche that you are not only good enough, but that you can do what you set out to do. Why would you want to shortchange yourself that? Instead, choose a sense of accomplishment, pride, and self-love. Remind yourself when you just want *a little break* that the risk of self-sabotage is great but the feeling from staying the course is even greater.

Since we are on the topic of acknowledgement, today you are going to turn back to your Day 1 pre-writing exercise, question #7. Who would you like to dedicate your book to? Who did you write down? Insert the title, *Dedication*, right before Chapter 1 in your Word document, then write a simple dedication. After that, I'd like you to then put together your acknowledgment page. Type *Acknowledgement* followed by those that you would like to thank for their encouragement, support, or inspiration for your writing. Again, if you get stuck on what other authors typically write, go to your bookshelf and review the acknowledgment pages in a handful of books.

I must tell you, there is something inspirational about developing the content for your acknowledgement. When you focus on gratitude for others, it opens you up to an inspirational and creative space. I am purposely having you do this on the day that you are to complete Chapter 8 because after today, you will only have four more days of writing. This dose of gratitude is going to have you focusing on the big, bright light at the end of the tunnel. Yes, you are so incredibly close! Writing your acknowledgement makes it feel super close and it will give you the inspiration and energy to give it everything you've got all the way to the finish line.

Now you are ready to review yesterday's writing and then complete Chapter 8. After you are done, I'd like you to write a few kinds words to yourself in your writing journal. I'd like you to tell yourself how proud you are that you have just completed eight chapters and that you have just two more to go. I'd like you to tell yourself that you knew that you could do it. After you finish writing your self-praise, place your hand on your heart and read what you wrote out loud. The mind body connection of this exercise is life-changing. I encourage you to use this process anytime you are nearing the finish line on something that you have committed to do as it will help cement into your subconscious that you can do anything.

Alright, I hope you are excited about today's writing. I'm excited for you!

DAY 20

We won't be distracted by comparison if we are captivated with purpose.
~ Bob Goff

Did you find an editor? Have you already sent off your prior chapters? Remember, you need to have found an editor and began the editing of your book by today. We only have 10 days until publication. There is no time to waste.

The editing of your book should not be taken lightly. A well edited book is worth its weight in gold. Even if you have a solid grasp on grammar and punctuation, a second or even third set of eyes to review your work will pay off. Just think of how many professionally edited books that you have read in your lifetime that have errors. Textbooks are notorious for having errors. This seems crazy since these are academic in nature. The point is that it is really easy to skim past grammatical errors, especially when you are familiar with what you meant to say. Your brain doesn't even see the misspelled or missing words. This is why you need another set of eyes.

I found editors through Fiverr.com at varying rates. What's most important is their turn around time because you are on a compressed timeline to get this book done. There are other freelance sites as well, such as Upwork.com. These freelance sites include bios of hundreds of freelancers in many areas of expertise. The areas that you will be most interested in finding freelancers for this project will be editing and cover design. If you decide to develop a website or need business promotional items designed, you will find these types of websites an extremely valuable resource. It's an amazing virtual marketplace.

Your book editing needs to be completed so that your cover design can be finalized. I will go into this more tomorrow, but this is why you will need to begin your editing by today. Most editors can turn around your work in less than three days, and many 24 hours if you are sending one chapter at a time.

Success Tip: When looking for an editor, in addition to the types of projects they typically do, price, and levels of services offered, you will want to make sure they can meet your timeline.

Today you will begin writing Chapter 9 and you will finish Chapter 10 by Day 23. If your first eight chapters are edited by Day 22 or 23 then it is a realistic expectation that your editor can turn around your final two chapters within a 24-hour period. Lay out this plan to your editor now, so that he or she knows what you are expecting. Keeping to this tight timeline is key to publishing on Day 30.

At this point you are nearing completing of writing the chapters of your book, which seems pretty amazing seeing that less than three weeks ago, this was merely a dream. Although we only have two more chapters to write, there is quite a bit of work to do between now and publishing. Please be extra diligent to stay on task with each of the additional daily activities that I have laid out. Every day you have an additional activity and your writing to complete, but this is the FUN part.

Before you begin writing today, if you have not settled on an editor, that is your first task. You will need to select an editor and send your editor Chapters 1-8. Next, you are going to download a formatted book template from Amazon's Kindle Direct Publishing (KDP) Help pages:

Paperback and Hardcover Manuscript Templates
URL: https://kdp.amazon.com/en_US/help/topic/G201834230
Select 'Choose a Template'. I like to use (Templates with sample content) because it makes it easier to cut and paste in each chapter.

Download the template in the formatted size that you like (I prefer 9 x 6") and Save the formatted template to your computer. Once you have edited chapters back you are going to start cutting and pasting your chapter content into the template. This is when this project starts to get REALLY exciting! Once you see your book starting to take shape into the formatted document, your dream shifts to reality. It's a really cool feeling and this will really drive you over the next week as we finish things up.

Building a Bridge

Now on to that little writing task. Chapter 9 is a pretty important chapter, as you are really bringing on home the rest of the content and it can be a bit tricky. Chapter 10 wraps everything into a neat package, but Chapter 9 is leading the reader up to the tippy-top of the mountain. I like to think of Chapter 9 as the bridge lyrics in a song. It's not the melody and it's not the harmony, it is that cool set of lyrics or key change in between. The bridge of a song typically helps the listener transition to the climactic point of the song – everything comes together because of the bridge. This is Chapter 9.

How do the notes on your Chapter 9 index cards serve as a bridge? How can you link your concepts or stories? Chapter 9 is an opportunity for you to really wow your readers. When well written, I have found that the next to the last chapter in fiction is one where you don't want to stop for the night; you want to power through.

Today, instead of focusing on word count—no, you aren't getting away from your minimum word count—focus on your bridge. If you need inspiration, listen to a few of your favorite songs and listen how the bridge transports you from one place to the next in the song. Help your readers take that journey! Remember, today is Part I of your bridge as today and tomorrow you will be working on your Chapter 9 bridge chapter. Tomorrow will be Part II.

Now it's time to review. Get inspired through your favorite music and then get to work. 5, 4, 3, 2, 1!

The only boundaries that exist are the ones
that you choose to create.

DAY 21

Believe you can and you're half way there.~ Theodore Roosevelt

How did your bridge building go yesterday? Did you get a good start? Think of your construction like building a great suspension bridge—like the Golden Gate Bridge in San Francisco, California. There are pylons driven 110 feet below the surface of the water. Tall stances hold suspension cables which link the massive, expansive structure together. Part I of your bridge is the foundational support pieces and today you will link everything together with Part II. Before we get started, let's talk about your book cover.

I asked you in an earlier chapter to think about your book cover and to investigate the covers of other books that catch your eye. You compiled a folder of ideas. You should have put some thought into the elements of your back cover and compiled those as well. Are you planning on providing prospective readers with a short synopsis of the book on the back? An author photo? Perhaps a few endorsements?

If you plan on having endorsements, you need to have them in by Day 25 so hop to it. Perhaps you are a bit apprehensive about asking someone for an endorsement, or you just don't know what to say. Let me begin by telling you that there are many people out there that love to support the dreams of others and would be more than happy to provide an endorsement. Book endorsements can come from many sources. As I stated previously, business colleagues or business professionals that friends or family are connected with, local service clubs, newspapers/magazines, church, or school are all excellence sources to find potential book endorsers.

When approaching someone for an endorsement, be confident and excited in your work. Whether you have an opportunity to ask in person, over the phone, or via email, share with that person that you are really excited about finishing this project and let them know that you are looking for people who would be willing to write a one or two sentence praise or endorsement for your book. Say, "I think you would be an ideal person because.... (state your reason why). I'd be truly honored if you would be willing to do this and of course, I'd make sure that you get a free copy of my book." Explain that you can provide them with 2-4 chapters to review so that they can write a few lines of praise. Of course, you are only going to provide edited chapters for their review. If they agree, let them know that you will need this back within just a few days as this is a 30-day project and reviews must be in by Day 25 for you to stay on track. Most people are going to be impressed by your commitment, and organization and will not only say yes to the endorsement, but also to helping you stay on track.

Two endorsements are usually plenty for the back cover. If you have a third, I would recommend this be a one-liner or concise and that this be placed on your front cover. This might read something like, "Emotional thriller! A must read! – The Press Telegram."

How will you be designing your cover? Are you willing or able to spend money to have your cover designed? If so, have you found someone on Fiverr, UpWork, or elsewhere? If you are unwilling or unable to spend money to have your cover designed, no worries, you can do this without any cost. A few questions will indicate how you will proceed from here. Are you able to use Photoshop or a similar program? Do you have a family member that has this skill and the computer program?

For the publication of your book, we will be using Amazon's KDP which has an online cover designer with standard templates that are absolutely free and do not require any design program knowledge. There is one drawback: the standard, canned cover designs will not allow for spine print for any book less than 100 pages. Spine print on a book is the title and author information up the spine of the book that would face out when on a bookshelf. The reason why spine print is important is if you ever want your book to be in a traditional bookstore, it will need to have spine print. If this isn't important to you and you just want to sell online or aren't really worried about selling books, then using one of KDP's cover designs will work well for you and it won't cost you a thing.

If you are designing your cover yourself or having someone else design your cover that is not familiar with KDP cover requirements (most Fiverr freelancers know KDP), you will need to download a cover template at:

https://kdp.amazon.com/en_US/cover-templates

You can get to work designing colors and layout, however the size of the spine and overall dimensions cannot be determined without an accurate page count. Once you have your edited chapters and have cut and paste into the book template, you will be able to determine the book cover dimensions from the page count formula.

If you are looking to use Fiverr or a similar freelance site, look for cover designers on Fiverr advertise that they will design your KDP or Amazon cover. The average cost for someone to design your cover on Fiverr is right around $150, yet there are some that will create your cover for $50. There are also many that will charge more and have additional offerings such as social media marketing pieces. Again, you don't have to spend a dime if you choose to use KDP's, in program cover designer.

You will need to have your cover designed and ready on Day 28 so come up with your game plan. Will you have endorsements? Who will you approach? Go out and get them. What's the worst they can say? No? When people tell me no, I like to make a game out of it and in my mind I say, "NEXT!", like I have a line waiting to endorse my work. 'No' certainly isn't the end of the world, because it only has the meaning that you give it. If you make 'no' a big deal, it will be. Why give it value? It's an opportunity for you to find someone even better that would be happy to support you.

Your cover design needs to be determined in short order, so put some thought into how you are going to approach this. If you plan to use one of KDPs free cover designs (there are quite a few to choose from) then you should only focus on your plan for what endorsements of information that you will be including on your front and back cover. Either way, on Day 28 we will have a finalized cover.

Bridge Completion

It's time to get back to that bridge you were building. What is your support system? Your job today is to connect your foundational piers with the support systems that will make a strong transition that folks will want to traverse to your next chapter. Your bridge completion will culminate with the conclusion of Chapter 9.

Just think, this is the first of your final three writing sessions before you complete your book. What are you waiting for? Review and write!

DAY 22

Greatness is not measured by what a man or woman accomplishes, but by the opposition he or she has overcome to reach the goal.

The final chapter. Yes! It's finally here. Today you will begin writing the final chapter of your book. Was writing a book as difficult as you once thought it would be? Along the way you have been working on pulling together additional information and getting prepared for the next step—publishing your book. I assure you, the final week will fly by and in another couple weeks, when you receive the first copy of your book in the mail, you will experience the greatest joy. Understanding the process will help you in other areas of your life wherein you may have felt less than confident.

It's pretty amazing how when we become enlightened, and given a plan, that we realize just how useless being fearful or having lack of confidence really is. We should all strive to be information seekers. This is your first line of defense against success blockers. From information we improve our level of knowledge and improve ourselves. Over the past three weeks, you have been improving your writing, your ability to follow through and your ability to follow instructions, all while working to make your dream come true.

The final chapter is your grand finale. What resounding message will you leave with your reader? Have you ever put down a book at completion and felt an instant sense of loss? It's almost like you just lost a dear friend and you are sad it has to come to an end. Have you ever waited for an author to release the next book in the series? A great story and a great message can have that effect on a reader.

Chapter 10 is your opportunity to leave your reader wanting more from you, but not leaving them feeling incomplete. If you are writing a book on weight-loss, your goal is to leave your readers feeling inspired to take action. If you are writing a romance, your goal is to leave your readers with an intense feeling. Whether that is happiness or sadness, that is up to you; just make sure to make the final message a strong one. Make sure that you don't leave your reader hanging. A saga is fine but there needs to be a sense of finality to define the end of the current writing. The *Harry Potter* series is a good example. Readers long for more but don't feel like they are dangling from a cliff.

When you developed your outline index cards, your tenth card may have just been a topic. You may not have thought of how that topic relates to or culminates from the other topics, characters, or stories. Some things to consider when building a strong conclusion and ending for your work is to have an idea of the end as you are writing. I like to say 'commit to your ending when you begin by committing to a message'. What is the meaning that you want to communicate from all of the pieces of the story or information? How will everything be linked together like the suspension cables on the bridge from Chapter 9? How will everything come together and make sense?

Look back through your previous chapters and seek opportunities to link concepts and stories. Maybe something that you introduced in an earlier chapter seemed complete within the context of what you presented in the earlier chapter but now you have a completely new context to reintroduce a twist or linkage into your final chapter. The goal here is to bring it all home. Everything should culminate into the grand finale.

Today is a really important writing day for you. The last chapter deserves all of your attention. For this reason, you have no other activities today outside of writing. I'd like you to dedicate extra time today to fully focus on developing a solid final chapter. This is the ONLY time in this entire writing project that I am going to give you permission to work straight through and complete the chapter if you are on a roll. This is up to you. Remember, you officially have one more day to complete Chapter 10 so if you need it, take that day. Keep in mind if you do complete your chapter today, you do not have a day off tomorrow. Did you actually think I would agree to that?

Now that you have your marching orders, get to work! Your task is to complete at least half of Chapter 10, if not all. Really enjoy today. Enjoy the amazing dedication and work that has brought you to this point. Pat yourself on the back, tap your chest with your finger and say, "You are one awesome author." Get writing. You got this.

Nothing will happen unless you take the initiative to do it.

Day 23

Happiness lies in the joy of achievement and the thrill of creative effort. ~
Franklin D. Roosevelt

Well, well, well, look at where you are! DAY 23 BABY! Yes! I know, I know, that's a whole lot of exclamation points, but heck, this is something to be using ALL CAPS and exclamation points over!!! This is it, the final writing day. As I stated yesterday, we have lots to do if you decided to push through and complete Chapter 10. If this remains your final writing day, you will be writing and working on some publishing items.

Yesterday I explained that Chapter 10 is the grand finale and I provided you with some ideas as to how to wrap prior concepts and stories up in a sensical manner. Today as you finish Chapter 10, I especially want you to focus on the very last paragraph and sentence. Your final thoughts, your concluding sentence, really think about the impact of your closing words. Then, step back for a moment, take your hands off your keyboard and think about what you have just done. You just wrote the final sentence to your book! In 23 days you wrote an entire book! In the time the average person might complete reading a book (about three weeks), you wrote a book. Now let's finish up this process and get you published.

As I explained, we are using Amazon's KDP platform to publish your book. Let me tell you that I am in no way connected to Amazon's KDP other than being an author like you. I am recommending KDP because I have found that it is an easy platform with all of the necessary resources for you to publish your first book. By using an all-inclusive platform like KDP, we take away excuses for not becoming published. There is no charge for you to publish your book on KDP, but you may choose to pay for a few items, depending on your end goal. Your first step will be to open a browser window and go to:

https://kdp.amazon.com/en_US/

From there you can set up your KDP account. Once you have that set up

Follow the prompts through "Create a New Title." You will be asked for your book title and author information. If you have a co-author or contributors, this is the page that you add this information. Next is the most critical piece of your book, the ISBN.

An ISBN, or International Standard Book Number, is a unique 10 digit number assigned to every published book. An ISBN identifies a title's binding, edition, and publisher. An EAN, or European Article Number, is a 13-digit number assigned to every book to provide a unique identifier for international distributors. The 10-digit ISBN is converted to a 13-digit EAN by adding a 978 prefix and changing the last digit.

You have a choice to either choose a KDP-assigned ISBN for free or you can choose to purchase an International ISBN for $125 from Bowkers at https://www.bowker.com/en/products-services/isbn-us/ Use the Order ISBN button at the top of the page to purchase your ISBN. If you choose to have KDP provide you with an ISBN, you will have a selection "Get a free KDP ISBN."

What's the difference in your own ISBN or the free version through KDP? The main difference is that this is where your end goal comes to play. A KDP-assigned ISBN will limit your publication to Amazon and its distribution. You will not be able to use any other publishing platform.

An International ISBN will give you the greatest flexibility if you want to place your books in retail stores or if you choose to publish on another platform. Some companies, Walmart, for example, will not consider selling KDP-assigned ISBN materials, mainly because they don't have access to order them. Keep this in mind when determining which ISBN is right for you. If you are okay with limiting your book to online sales on your website and through Amazon and its Expanded Distribution (worldwide), then don't worry about purchasing an ISBN. As I stated from the beginning, you can publish for nearly no cost.

Save your set up as a Draft. The interior file cannot be completed until your editing is done. That is why I had you download the template. If for some reason you did not do that, please download the formatted template so that you can get your book into the proper format. As you receive back your edited chapters, you can cut and paste them into the formatted chapter set up.

Once you are completed writing Chapter 10, send your final chapters off for editing. Remember, you must have these chapters back by Day 25. That's it for Day 23. That's it for the writing process. Now, for the next week we will be preparing your book for publication.

DAY 24

Who you are tomorrow begins with what you think today. ~ Jolene Church

Your writing is complete, and your editor is busy editing your work. When your work comes back, it will likely have redlined tracked changes. You can accept the suggested edits one change at a time or accept all and stop tracking under the "Review" tab in Word. I suggest that you read through the document and the suggested edits. Your editor may have a distinct style that he or she may want to introduce in the edits. You may want to pick and choose suggestions. However, if it appears that rather than style edits, the edits appear to mostly be punctuation and grammar, you may just choose to accept all edits and move on.

What I'd like you to do today, especially if you have not yet received back your early chapters from your editor, is to set up the introductory pages for your book. In the template you will see the information to fill in. You will prepare your Title Page with the book title and author. The next page is your copyright page. On this page, change the copyright date to the current year, add your author name, and your ISBN. Your book dedication page is next. Retrieve what you wrote during the writing process activities for both your dedication and your acknowledgements. You will cut and paste each into the template.

The cut and paste process of your chapter content into the template can be time consuming. You will cut and paste the text from one chapter at a time and put in the title of each chapter manually following the chapter number (if you have a chapter title- usually in non-fiction).

The table of contents can be cut out of the document if you do not have chapter titles and you do not wish to have a table of contents. I suggest you leave it, just because it makes it easier for the reader to reference each chapter starting page. If you do have chapter titles, in addition to adding the page numbers in the table of content, you will add the chapter titles as well.

Your final task for the day is to convert your ISBN into a barcode for the back cover of your book (only if you are using a purchased barcode). KDP will prompt you when adding your cover information: "Check this box if the cover you're uploading includes a barcode. If you don't check the box, we'll add a barcode for you. Learn more about barcode size and placement."

If you are purchasing your barcode, you can do this through Bowkers for $25. Your barcode should include the price of your book. Not sure how much your book should be? Look on Amazon or another online book retailer for books in your genre to determine the best price. I'd suggest that you keep you price your book somewhere between 10.99 and 16.99 depending on the page count and the price of comparable titles. Only compare prices of paperbacks.

There are several places you can go to convert your ISBN into a barcode, but I haven't found many free options. One free option is available at https://www.bookow.com/. I have used Bookow and your barcode will hit your email within seconds. Once you have your barcode, you are finished for the day.

Let me finish up this chapter by saying that I understand that patience is incredibly hard to exercise at this point as you go through this final week. It is so hard to contain the excitement and it's natural to want to rush through the process since you are so close. Believe me when I say that I know how you feel. I've been there, and I've learned to appreciate getting all of your ducks in a row in a systematic manner. I'm thrilled to guide your journey to the fulfillment of your dream. Just a few more days. Be proud of your accomplishment.

DAY 25

Never allow waiting to become a habit. Live your dreams and take risks. Life is happening now.

Today you should have all of your chapters back from your editor. You may have received some of your earlier chapters back and have begun cutting and pasting into the template. If not, today is the day to complete that task. This is also the day that will send you through the roof with excitement when you finish cutting and pasting into the book template. At the end of today's exercise, you should have a completed interior to your book.

After you cut and paste your edited chapter content, you will see that there is one final piece for your book after the last chapter, "About the Author". At this point, if you are not totally satisfied with the author bio that you created during your earlier assignment, work on your bio and then cut and paste it into the "About the Author" section at the end of the template. Save this document to your computer. This completes your book interior file. Note your page count. Your page count is important for your cover design as it needs to be an exact count.

Once your book interior is complete, give it a solid page-by-page review to make sure that you didn't accidentally leave an extra space between a paragraph or leave a title hanging at the bottom of the page. Review each page for errors and make any needed corrections. When you are satisfied, login to your KDP account and go to the "Interior" section of your project setup.

You will select your paper type. I suggest you use the black and white print and white paper options. Select the standard 6" x 9" book size option (assuming you chose the 6" x 9" template). Next, you will upload your book interior file (upload paperback manuscript). Browse for you book file that is save to your computer to upload it to KDP and select Save. KDP will then provide an automated print check. This check will identify any potential print issues. This may take several minutes.

Launch the interior viewer. This is perhaps the most exciting and important part of the process thus far. In the interior viewer mode, you will be able to flip through the pages of your book and review the content. Make sure that your chapters are beginning where you want them to as some books have chapters that start on both the left and right side of the page, whereas others will leave a blank page on the left to ensure that each chapter starts on the right side page inside the book.

The reality of what you have accomplished will really hit home at this point. You can choose to "Save and Continue" if you find no changes necessary or "Go Back and Make Changes." If you choose to go back and make changes, make the changes to the file on your computer and save the file with a version number, i.e. MyBookV2. Once you have made all the necessary changes you can go back through the steps of uploading your manuscript into KDP again.

Once you are satisfied with the interior review of your book, save and continue in KDP. The next item in the checklist is the " Book Cover." You can choose "Use Cover Creator to make your book cover" or you can choose to upload a print ready pdf cover that either you or your cover designer developed. The cover template for KDP can be located at:

https://kdp.amazon.com/en_US/cover-templates

If you are using a KDP designed cover, have fun selecting from the design options, one that best fits your book. Pay attention to the back cover real estate available on each of the cover options. If you have several cover endorsements, you will want to select the cover that will best accommodate your content. If you do not have endorsements, no worries, pull out the book synopsis that you wrote as a part of your writing exercises. See, I told you I had you covered!

Once you have a cover design, if you want KDP to assign your ISBN, don't check the box at the bottom of the Book Cover section. If you have decided to have a freelancer on Fiverr or another site design your cover and have found one that specifically advertises that they design KDP book covers, all you will need to provide is your ISBN barcode and your page count, along with design instructions. You will then check the box that says that your upload includes a barcode (otherwise KDP assigns you one). Remember that your cover design needs to be completed by Day 28. Happy designing.

Once you have a completed design today or by Day 28, upload your completed design file under the "Cover" option tab and Save.

Success is not final, failure is not fatal:
it is the courage to continue that counts.
~ Winston Churchill

DAY 26

Don't expect to see a change if you don't make one.

Spread the Word!

Let's talk about the future of your book. You are done writing. You have either begun designing your cover or are having someone else design it for you. You have had your work edited, have cut and pasted your chapter content into the template, and completed the interior of your book. Now what? That's the question of the day.

What do you want to do with your book? Are you wanting to sell your book on Amazon? Are you wanting to sell your book on your website? Or perhaps you want to do both. Or maybe for those of you who decided to purchase and ISBN, you want to figure out how to get in all of the major bookstores.

On your first day you answered a series of questions. Question #5 was, "Who would be interested in this book and why?" I later explained about knowing your target market so that you understand who your audience is and can identify ways to market specifically (targeted marketing) to those who would likely want to buy your book.

You will need to know your target market so that you can begin a social media campaign for your book right away. If you have already designed your cover, you can screenshot your book cover and use that photo to promote your "Soon to Be Released" social media announcement. If you don't yet have a cover design, you can use an online free design app, such as Canva to make a mock cover to promote your work in advance of your official cover being done. Just go to Canva and select book cover design, find a template that you like, fill in your title and author information and save as a JPEG or GIF file.

If selling tons of books is your goal, then you will need to start marketing ASAP! You can have your friends share your posts and get the word out. If you can get an "influencer" on a social media site to share your posts, even better. Anywhere you can post information for free, I suggest you do so as soon as possible. Social media is a given for promoting but don't forget about other places, such as any clubs or groups that you belong to.

Check with local mom and pop book stores to ask if, when your book is released, they would be interested in having you come to do an author reading. Let them know that you will give them a percentage of any books sold while you are there for the reading and that you will sign any books purchased that day (if you use a free ISBN). If you did not get a free ISBN, the store will be able to order you books once your title data is submitted to Bowkers. Book clubs are another good source for marketing your work.

I'd be remiss if I did not tell you about Goodreads. Goodreads, if you are unfamiliar, is a social cataloguing website for people to search through digital book catalogs. Individuals can interact with authors and fellow readers through blog posts and surveys. As an author, you can set up an author page and build a following much like Facebook or Twitter. You can also set up book giveaways to generate interest in your book. I suggest signing up for Goodreads and checking it out.

Distribution and Royalties

Now let's discuss book sales. In particular, online book sales. By publishing through the KDP platform, you can sell your book on Amazon and its worldwide Expanded Distribution network. You may also develop a Kindle version of your book for sale as well. I personally love Amazon's Expanded Distribution. With Expanded Distribution, your book can be sold to participating online and brick and mortar book retailers at wholesale prices. For additional information about distribution and sales options login to your KDP account and navigate to the "Channels" tab under "Distribute" in the tool bar on the left side of your project screen.

Once you have had an opportunity to review sales options, it's probably the perfect time to start talking about costs and royalties. By publishing your book through KDP, your book will be printed on-demand. That means that once your book is published, it is not sitting in a warehouse somewhere. Instead, it remains a digital file until someone orders a copy. Once an order is placed through Amazon the book is printed. You can also order author copies at "cost." Your *cost to print* will display on the screen as you set up distribution in KDP.

The cost of your book will vary based on the page count of your book, assuming you went with the standard size, print, and paper color options that I suggested. If your book is in the range of 115-200 pages, your book will probably be somewhere around $4 per copy wholesale (cost). This is the price you pay from Amazon, plus any applicable tax and shipping. The retail price that you put on your ISBN is the price Amazon will charge others (retail) for your book.

A royalty is the amount that Amazon will pay you for your book. Once your book set up is complete, you will be able to see royalty amounts for each distribution channel. If you book is priced somewhere between $12.99 and $15.99, and your book falls in line with about a $4 wholesale cost, your royalty will likely be somewhere between $4-7 per sale on Amazon (paperback). Keep in mind that all of the costs that I am giving you are educated guesses based on my experience. Your actual figures may be different. Once you get your book set up, you will have a solid set of figures as you can see what your royalties will be during your distribution set up. The percentage of sales royalties that you receive (up to 70%), depend on the distribution option that you choose during setup.

If you decide to also publish to Kindle, which you can do as a final step of the publishing process, keep in mind that although your royalties will be very small on these sales, there are no printing costs. By having both Kindle and print, you will expand buyer options. If you aren't interested in publishing to Kindle, you can skip the Kindle set up step, which mimics the paperback set up steps.

If you are going to be selling books from your website, you can do one of two things. You can purchase from KDP, hold your own inventory, and ship when you receive orders, or you can link your site to your Amazon products page. There are advantages to both. I sell way more books myself than I do on Amazon because I sell them at my events. When I sell my own products, I maximize my profits. I'm buying at cost and selling at retail. I can also offer discounts and incentives to seminar and conference attendees. If you sell through Amazon, buyers are able to leave product reviews, and you will build a sales ranking. This is important if you are considering attracting a traditional publisher in the future.

Today is all about thinking about your marketing and sales strategy. By tomorrow, you will be promoting today's work on social media. If you aren't on social media, this is the time to set yourself up on Facebook, Instagram, and Twitter. Set up your Goodreads account. If you do not have your cover design completed, develop a mock cover design using Canva or a similar web-based program so that you will have a book cover photo just for marketing. It's okay that this differs from your actual book cover. You can re-post your actual cover when your design is finished. Brainstorm on paper as many ideas about how you can share information with friends, family, community, and your immediate social network (church, clubs, etc.). We will visit this idea list tomorrow.

DAY 27

You only live once, but if you do it right, once is enough. ~Mae West.

Today is marketing day. Every idea that you had yesterday will come to life today. Today is a day of action. You will write emails, make phone calls, talk to people in person, and promote your work on social media. Today is the day we start spreading the word.

Tomorrow you will have your final cover design ready and we will be on the fast-track to proofing and finalizing your publication. You may have your cover design back and are ready to go, but under any typical conditions (not during a 30 day writing and publishing challenge), this marketing effort typically would have started months ago. Since you began writing your book less than a month ago, we must focus on this VERY necessary step now, while we have a moment before publication.

Your assignment yesterday was to set up your social media accounts, if you didn't already have them. You should have also created your Goodreads account profile and set up an author dashboard. The final item that you were to complete was a marketing idea list. What did you come up with? Who did you come up with?

You should now have some sort of image of either your actual or mock book cover. You are going to post to social media by adding the photo and letting the social media community know that your book is about to be released!

Hype it Up

Question #3 on Day 1 was "My book is about...." This was your writing prompt for your book promotion. Now, it's highly likely that what you wrote on the first day is not exactly ready to be blasted out to social media without some polishing. Look over what you wrote as if you were in a book store, reading the back-cover book synopsis. Would what you wrote entice you to buy that book? If not, revise what you wrote to sell someone on your book. If you have a tough time, go back to Day 4 when I asked you to "sell your book"; this may help get you on the right track. When you complete your sales pitch, post the write-up along with your book cover photo. Make sure you have an eye-catching title for your write-up, such as, "RELEASING SOON-An Amazing Tale of Courage."

Let your audience know how they can get updates on the status of your book release. Do you have a website? Do you have a mailing list? Let people know what they should do next. Your marketing pitch is your call to action. Consider a giveaway or drawing. Start building up the excitement around the release of your book.

I said previously that you would be calling, emailing, and contacting people today. If you put it on your idea list, you need to make things happen. This might mean that you may be running down to your neighborhood bookstore and asking the store owner if they will help you promote your work by allowing you to come do a book reading in a few weeks. This may mean that you will be distributing flyers to your church, at your gym, on bulletin boards at the coffee shop or laundromat, promoting you work and driving traffic to your website for more information. Your sole job today is to HYPE-IT-UP! Get out of your comfort zone. The choice you decide not to make may be the choice that was needed to be successful. Do not look at asking others to help promote your work as embarrassing or like you are asking for the moon. You are asking for them to be a part of your success. Do not underestimate the power of networking. It is essential in marketing your work.

Today is your call to action. Go create some excitement! Hype it up!

DAY 28

Why fit in when you were born to stand out? ~ Dr. Seuss

I'd say that this is the day that you have been waiting for, but it's just one of many. Today you have all of the pieces to put your book together. You have a completed interior and a completed cover.

If you did not produce a cover through KDP, you will follow the prompts through uploading your cover. You can launch the viewer from the Preview Tab to see what the book would look like both outside and inside. You will see a summary box at the bottom that shows the specifics of your book (ink and paper type, bleed setting, trim size and page count). If you are satisfied, hit Save to move on. If you need to make changes to your cover or book interior, you can redo your files, re-upload and re-preview. Your cost to print will show up in the summary. Once you are satisfied with both the interior and exterior, click the Save and Continue button at the bottom.

Now is the time for you to set up your distribution channels. Under the "Pricing" tab you can review and select your distribution channels to see your royalties based on the price of your book in various areas around the world. Choose the royalty option that appeals most to you.

Finally, accept the Terms and Conditions. The last piece You are just about to the finish line. The final item that you have been waiting for – if you have completed all steps – Click Publish Your Paperback Book.

Keep in mind that your job is not over. Once submitted, your book could take up to 72 hours to show up on Amazon. It's important that you continue building the excitement around your book.

You just hit the PUBLISH button! Go celebrate while you wait for it to go live. Use the excited energy to market, market, market!

DAY 29

Perseverance is not a long race; it is many short races one after the other.
~ Walter Elliot

Today is all about finalizing everything that you have put into place. For the past several weeks, you have been working diligently toward seeing a dream come to fruition. I'm sure that you have experienced days throughout this process that you questioned whether the task that you set out to do could truly come to be. Had you not entertained a thought that you could, an ounce of hope and belief in yourself, you would not be sitting here today, awaiting the message from KDP that your book is live on Amazon.

What you have accomplished and experienced is something that will help you through anything that you desire to accomplish in the future. The most important thing that you have done is to give yourself the okay to fail. You thought, "Why not? I've always wanted to do this," and you decided to take the first step. You then took multiple steps, on a path that you were unsure where it led; but you did it anyway.

We are programmed to avoid failure. Fail = Bad. Failure is not bad. Failure means that you tried. Without having many failures in our life, we would never experience the beauty of succeeding. For any of you that meet the criteria, that I heard from thousands of people, and that prompted me to write this book, "I've been working on writing and compiling a book for years." Embracing failing as a good thing, as a necessary step that we must master on our way to success. You now can look back at all the time that you spent writing and compiling, as well as the times you didn't get done what you wanted to, as a good thing. What you accomplished led to your accomplishment AND what you did not accomplish also led to your accomplishment – because you learned, adjusted, re-committed and persevered.

I believe the editing process can be one of the hardest things to come to grips with, especially if your editor tears apart your writing style. Embrace the opportunity to succeed. Every learning experience gets you one step closer to eventual success.

Mastering failing is one of the best things that you can do for yourself. During this process, did you have days that you slacked off? Bravo! What did you learn from that? Did it extend a day or two or more? Did you get a week or two in and then put down your writing and check out for a while? Or did you power through, but had days that were less productive than others? Everything that missed your expectations can be chalked up as a fail, and that is a good thing!

This writing project is proof-positive that succeeding is a part of your DNA. We are all naturally created to succeed. Our choices to step beyond our comfort zone and step out in faith and willingness to fail along the way to success—getting back up when we fall down and realizing that it is simply a step toward learning how to walk. Soon, when your book is in your hand, you will have established a new belief system, that you can do whatever you set your mind to.

Today is a day of waiting. You are waiting on a message from KDP. Check your email. Do you have a message yet from KDP that your book is live?

Once you receive the email notifying you that your book is live, you can order, at cost, author copies. You can do this by going to your KDP Bookshelf and hitting the three dots to the far right of the screen next to your book. These will be added to an Amazon cart just like if you were ordering anything else on Amazon except you won't see the price displayed. Just select the quantity that you want to order and when you add to your cart and select your shipping option you will see your total price. Remember, you are paying wholesale (cost to print) plus shipping and any applicable taxes.

Congratulations, you are now a published author! Would you like to also publish on Kindle? If you haven't already, follow the steps on your main Bookshelf page, Create a New Title – Kindle eBook. This is optional. Kindle will open you up to more readers, but the royalties are much less as your pricing is less. You can always choose to publish on Kindle later.

If you purchased your ISBN through Bowkers, you have one final step and that is to assign your Book Title Data to associate your ISBN with the information about your book. This step is crucial for purchased ISBN titles to show up in Bowker's Books in Print. This is a database that retailers use to purchase your book for their stores. Under My Account - Manage ISBN – click your title and fill out the data sheet. You will select Active Record for status before you submit. It takes about 5 days for retailers to be able to see the data. If you used KDPs ISBN, no worries, everything is done for you.

Now that your book is published, it's time to pour on the marketing! Keep in mind that reviews on Amazon are only for those who have purchased your book through Amazon. If you are selling your author copies, your fans can't leave reviews. They can, however, leave a review on your website or on Goodreads. Reviews help drive future purchases, so encourage anyone that you know that purchases your book to provide you with a review.

Finally, if you order wholesale, your shipment takes longer than if you ordered off of Amazon or with Prime. If you just can't wait, order yourself a copy off of Amazon at full price. I think it's worth getting a book in your hands as quickly as possible. I'm excited for you. When that shipment comes, I want to hear from you.

DAY 30

Nothing builds self-esteem and self-confidence like accomplishment.
~ Thomas Carlyle

Well, well my fellow author, if you went through the proofing process without any delays and resubmissions, you are done. You have ordered copies of your book and you are ready to go into full-bore marketing mode. If you have some design or formatting issues to contend with and you still have to resubmit, you will be at this place shortly, but you can still market like crazy!

If you are done, you are thinking, "Wait a minute, this book was titled, How to Write and Publish a Book in 30 Days, not 28 or 29 days". This is because 30 days is more believable. My work as a success coach has been built upon helping break down barriers to people's thinking. Realistically, with some extra heavy-duty work, you could have completed this book in about 25 days. Instead, I pushed you, but not so hard that you would feel that you couldn't. The only barrier to not completing in 30 days is self-imposed, but as we learned, failing is also succeeding, because you learn.

Bottom-line, what I want you to take away from this book and this process is that your thoughts determine your destiny. Your thoughts determine your perception. You only feel a certain way about anything because you choose to feel that way. You believed that you could, and you did. You stepped out in faith, even though you may have thought "it's impossible." The only impossible things are what you believe are impossible.

You can change your thinking and change your life, and you have! What will you accomplish next? Most importantly, who will you inspire to help change their life?

I've written this book hoping to encourage and inspire you to see beyond the unseen and to help you achieve your dreams. I have written this book to help you turn impossible into possible. Never stop dreaming. Never stop believing. You were created to succeed. Now, continue to make it happen.

ABOUT THE AUTHOR

Dr. Jolene Church is the founder and CEO of Dr. Jolene Church Success Coaching, where she helps to inspire passion, confidence and authenticity in her clients by helping them define and live in their purpose, on purpose.

Dr. Church is an accomplished speaker, best-selling author, success coach, author incubator and human resources professional.

When Jolene isn't busy writing, creating, or coaching, the native Californian enjoys golfing with her hubby, riding on the back of his Harley, or enjoying a great glass of wine.

WWW.DRJOLENECHURCH.COM

For more information on success coaching, workshops, or other publications, please visit www.drjolenechurch.com.